MW00946676

Contentment in Contentious Times
The Secret of the Shepherd

Melissa ♥
Listen for His voice!

By
Dana Gailey

Dana Gailey
6/22

To Jesus, my good Shepherd,
Whose voice leads me to contentment in Him.

Contentment in Contentious Times: The Secret of the Shepherd
Copyright © 2016 by UImpact Publishing
All Rights Reserved

No part of this book may be used, reproduced, uploaded, stored or introduced into a retrieval system, or transmitted in any way or by any means (including electronic, mechanical, recording, or otherwise), without the prior written permission of the publisher, with the exception of brief quotations for written reviews or articles. No copying, uploading, or distribution of this book via the Internet is permissible.

The author, writers, and publisher have made every effort to include accurate information and website addresses in this work at the time of publication, and assume no responsibility for changes, omissions, inaccuracies, or errors that occur before or after publication. The publisher does not endorse or assume responsibility for the information, author, and writer websites, or third-party websites, or their content.

Contentment in Contentious Times: The Secret of the Shepherd

Religion / Christian Life / Spiritual Growth

E-book Version: Kindle
ISBN-10: 1536863548
ISBN-13: 978-1536863543
Religion / Christian Life / Spiritual Growth

CONTENTS

Part 1: The Search for Contentment

Part 2: The Battle for Contentment

Part 3: Pray Without Ceasing

Introduction

We can spend our lives looking for contentment in the accumulation of stuff and the security money brings, in relationships and expectations we have of others or ourselves, or in our experiences and accomplishments. I have certainly found a sense of contentment in living the good life in the United States of America. But if our circumstances have to line up with our expectations before we are content in Christ, we miss today and the richness God intends for us.

Think of those we know who are discontent with their lives. Discontentment is not the sorrow of grief from loss or deep need. Discontentment is not chronic physical or emotional pain. We walk through sorrow, loss, and illness with trust that God will bring us through, but discontentment is a different struggle. Restless discontent makes us look for love in all the wrong places as we continually wait for our circumstances to line up with our expectations of life.

Moments of discontentment can turn into years, then into decades and finally into a lifetime of one disappointment after another. Yet Paul the apostle who was beaten with rods, stoned, and shipwrecked taught us that there is a secret to contentment. It is not found in circumstances but in listening for the voice of and following our Good Shepherd. Paul had learned that contentment has less to do with circumstances or what's going on in the world around us than with whose voice we are listening to.

Paul had learned that he was flawed, loved, *and* had purpose. The power of God's love had transformed his life, and his purpose was to relay that message to a hurting world. We, too, are flawed, much loved, and have been transformed by God's love. Paul's purpose is our purpose.

Now, a grandma, I'm spoiled. I like my filtered water, hot baths, skin care, supplements, and plenty of sleep. I like to turn on a heater to get warm and an air conditioner to cool off. I enjoy having favor with people. When I love them they usually, not always, but usually love me back. I'm also a proud American. I love knowing my family is secure, that my husband and I and most of our children and grandchildren are healthy, love the Lord, love us, and love each other. But must I have these things in place for contentment? Shouldn't I, who have so much, be content?

I should be.

Yet the good, safe life and getting to do things our way is not what makes for contentment. If perfectly amiable circumstances made for contentment, what in the world happened to Eve? What about Solomon, the wisest and richest man in the world? It is sad to say, but what God has given us much of the time is just not enough. Like Eve and Solomon, when we listen to the lies of the deceiver we stray from the voice of our loving Shepherd. And when we stray from God's voice, we want that next thing just beyond our grasp, and then the next.

Ever discontent.

This is the fight.

Through these pages may we find that *secret* place Paul knew of and learn how to fight for the contentment every heart longs for. *Especially* in these contentious times.

Part 1
The Search for Contentment

1

My Days – All His

"This is the day the Lord has made. I will rejoice
and be glad in it"
…because it is all His.

Today.
> This is the day.
>> The only day we have.
>>> Yet, how often we miss it.

I think back to a day years ago when I held my baby, just six weeks old, for what seemed forty-eight hours. We had walked, rocked, bounced, and cuddled. Then I laid him in his bed once again and let him cry. It was a stifling July afternoon. I stepped out on the porch, put my face in my hands, and sobbed, "Help me, Lord."

This was the beginning of my journey with Jesus. I was a new Christian, a fresh bloom. I was trying to listen for the voice of my Shepherd, whatever that meant. I was also a new mommy learning to care for my first baby boy. My mother, sister and sisters-in-law lived hundreds of miles away, and I knew only one new mommy. Until the day I brought Christopher home I thought with pride, *Women have been taking care of babies since the garden. This will be a piece of cake, right?*

Wrong. In those first weeks of motherhood I learned why sleep deprivation is a means of torture. I was sleep-deprived, bedraggled, and smelled like baby throw up. Though feeding this little guy was one of the sweetest times of my life, it was sometimes painful and humiliating. My milk dropped when I was in the checkout line at the grocery store but not when the baby was hungry. He often fell asleep before he was full and woke up crying. And one of our greatest challenges was burp time. I could not get that boy to burp! After he ate and fell asleep (without burping) I would gingerly lay him down. But before I could get a thing done or a wink of sleep he would wake up screaming drawing his little legs up to the bubble in his tummy. More than once his spit-ups splattered on the wall. I thought he was dying.

I went to one of those La Leche League meetings held in a tiny room stuffed with sweaty mommies and babies. Those women were a little too "flower-child" for me so I never went back. Had I swallowed my pride and stuck with it, I probably wouldn't have found myself in this dilemma. Christopher was exhausted and hungry, and I was exhausted and bewildered.

Since I had been a little girl getting out of bed at night to cover up my dollies and stuffed animals, I had longed to be a mommy. Yet here I was sweating bullets and bawling on the porch. I felt like a failure. Though I loved this precious life more than my own, this mommy job was a lot harder than I thought it would be. I had a learning curve to navigate but had not yet learned to be content when I didn't know what was around that curve. I had no idea that this would be one of the smaller learning curves of the life ahead of me.

No, I had not yet learned to listen for the voice of my Shepherd. I knew nothing of the *secret* Paul wrote about to the Philippians. All I knew to do was to cry, "Help me, Lord." That's where I started and it is often my simple cry today.

We can't see around those curves, can we? We learn as we go. That's the way God set it up. The more we do things the better we become at doing them. Eventually sweet Christopher had a mommy who figured out what she was doing—most of the time. I learned to get a burp out of any baby you handed me and knew without a doubt that sleep deprivation would not kill me. So in the middle of the night, instead of wondering how I would function the next day with so little sleep, I enjoyed alone time—just baby and me.

I had not yet learned that there is beauty and design in *each day*, that life has seasons, and each is unique. I didn't know as I was growing, learning, and changing that I wouldn't know a lot of things. And that's OK!

I was one of God's lambs and He was leading me on a journey. Only He knew where the valleys, mountain tops, and the bends in the road were going to be. Though I did not know the way, He did. I didn't realize that discontent began in the Garden with that gal who nursed *her* first baby. It began because instead of listening to the voice of her beloved Father, her Shepherd, and keeping her heart close to her husband's, she listened to the voice of a stranger who was a deceiver.

Love the One in Front of You

Today is unique. It may be enjoyable, mundane, difficult, or seemingly impossible. Our purpose in this day like all others though, is to follow Jesus our Shepherd and let His love shine through us to our hurting world—the world right in front of us. We won't walk this way again. We don't get a do-over. The solution is simple then: **Love the one in front of you.**

Simple, but *not easy*. Whoever's in front of me needs to see God's love in me so they will wonder what it is and want some. Because Jesus the Shepherd is guiding me, every appointment is a divine appointment. If I am listening for His voice, no matter how those appointments turn out, I know my Shepherd has led me that way. God has this thing! My day has purpose! In knowing He has a purpose in my days I find contentment.

Believing God has purpose in my days is easy, but living like it is not. Therein lies the fight. The devil uses fear, distraction, disappointment, embarrassment, and discouragement to keep us from impacting our world right where we are. We hold back in fear or lash out in impatience and frustration. He wants us to be so *self-absorbed* that we miss the greater picture. The greater picture is the world around us desperately looking for love—those who are right in front of us. I disappoint myself and others when I don't love the face in front of me.

Wherever You Are, Be There

Regarding loving the one in front of me, some of the best advice I ever received was, "Wherever you are, be there." Wherever I am, hauling hay, changing a diaper, working at a job, fixing dinner, caring for an elderly parent, feeding the dog, in the checkout line, buying car insurance, taking out the garbage, or slapping together a sandwich for my family—I need to be there.

To love the person in front of me.

Life is simpler, easier, and more manageable when I remember to live right where I am and love the person in front of me. Most days in this season of my life, the person in front of me is my husband, Don. I have been known to use sarcasm to make a point (a sin), and fatigue makes cowards of us all (sin). A sarcastic coward (a sinner) does not pass the kindness test. But when I choose to be kind, I am doing my best job for me, for Jesus, and for my world. The rumpled note on my refrigerator is true: "Whoever I am at home is who I am. Life makes up its mind at home."

The good news: The things I struggle with at home are those very things God wants to deal with in my heart. In those areas are learning curves He wants to take me around, if I will let Him. He is leading me to grow and change to look more like Him day by day.

The bad news: Until I make those curves, those I love most take the hit.

When Don asks loudly from the next room for the fourth time, "What did you say?" my flesh wants to scream! But *through Christ* I can wash the raw meat off my hands, turn down the bubbling on the stove, and with patient love go in and talk to the man—just being kind. After all he's the one in front of me.

On the outside, this looks like a *yes face*.

A *YES Face* in a No World

I taught school until the day Christopher was born and went back into teaching when the boys were three, five, and eight. I loved teaching history and literature most of all, so I grew to love the short stories in our literature books. One story in the third grade reader that captured my heart was about Theodore Roosevelt. This was a man who lived his life to the fullest. A statesman and an adventurer, at 42 Theodore was thrust into the Presidency of the United States when Grover Cleveland was assassinated. He had moved around a great many learning curves by the time he became President. He had experienced many adventures including the famous charge up San Juan Hill. This colorful historical figure had overcome many sorrowful days, as well. Out of sheer determination he overcame severe physical limitations, and perhaps the greatest sorrow he overcame was when both his first wife and mother died on the same day.

The setting of this story was one of his infamous hunting expeditions. A guide and his young son led the President and his party out to the wilderness for the hunt. While riding along, the boy's horse bucked him into the dirt and ran away. Before any in the group had an opportunity to react, the boy was sitting behind the President. There he rode back to camp. When the hunt concluded and the President's party left, the astonished guide asked his son why he had climbed onto the President's horse. The boy replied, "I looked up at everyone, Papa, and President Roosevelt was the only one with a *yes face.*"

A *yes face*. I like that.

Whether I like Roosevelt's propensity for big game hunting or not, from Teddy I learned what a *yes face* is. Not surprisingly he was a man who read his Bible. We see the value he put in God's word when he said, "A thorough knowledge of the Bible is worth more than a college education." and "(It is) necessary for the welfare of the nation that men's lives be based on the principles of the Bible." He was right. God's sweet word in him and listening for the voice of the Shepherd was no doubt the power behind the *yes face* that the guide's son looked up and saw on Roosevelt that day. His *yes face* beamed from deep inside.

My Facebook face is all smiles without the blood, sweat, and tears behind them. However, those of us who know of the wonder of God's love and seek to listen for His voice, can have an authentic *yes face*, a face that shows the Shepherd's love smiling from deep inside us. Loving the one God has put in front of me today and letting my *yes face* shine might touch one heart *or* it might touch ten! Touching hearts takes me beyond myself and my circumstances and gives me purpose and contentment.

Not a *YES* Face

A young friend who works in a local restaurant informed me that the servers she works with hate the Sunday crowd. It's obvious to anyone in the restaurant business where the Sunday crowd has been on Sunday morning. In her experience the folks who go out to eat after church are often the most demanding and condescending of the week. They are also cheap! That made me sad.

Everyone is looking for a *yes face*— **a face that says, I care about you.** The Sunday crowd (that's us!) should take a *yes face* with us wherever we go. In this "no" world, we should be the face of Jesus: patient, gracious, *and* generous tippers! I would love to tell you that I always have on a *yes face*. Because I am a sinner and my efforts apart from Christ are fruitless, that is not true. I aspire with God's sweet grace though; to be a person whose face shows a heart of contented love. When I show my world a *yes face*, I am listening to my Shepherd and allowing Him to love through me, even if times are frustrating, scary, or confusing.

When we feel the need to be condescending or demanding we are displaying something wanting in us, perhaps contentment. Intentionally walking out our purpose and treating others with kindness whether they reciprocate or not is why God has us on the planet. There is no better time than Sunday for the Sunday crowd to have faces that say, "I follow a Shepherd who loves me. He loves you too"

Paul called it a secret.

The Secret

Paul had learned a secret and wrote to the Philippians. "I have learned to be content whatever the circumstances. I know what it is to be in need and I know what it is to have plenty. I have learned the secret of being content in every situation whether well fed or hungry, whether living in plenty or want. I can do all things through Christ who gives me strength" (Philippians 4: 11-13).

"I can do all things through Christ who gives me strength" is a verse that has sustained men and women of God through wars and horrific circumstances. It reminds us that when we are weak He is strong in us. In context though, Paul was talking about being content in no matter what circumstance he found himself. Paul, like Jesus and many of us, understood the dark ache of rejection. He had been beaten to a bloody pulp, left for dead, and thrown out of almost every town he entered. A lot of people hated him, but Paul didn't care. He had learned the secret of being content.

Eve had it all, and she was discontent. The difference was, Paul listened to God. Eve listened to the voice of a stranger. Paul also knew that we are engaged in a deadly war. Even though he was abused and his stomach was at times empty, he had learned to recognize God's voice. He truly believed, "The Lord is my Shepherd. I shall not want" (Psalm 23:1). The NIV reads, "The Lord is my Shepherd. I lack nothing!"

David, the shepherd king, wrote those words in Psalm 23. He knew the heart of a shepherd and the habits and behavior of sheep. So he knew that though many voices may call out to a herd of sheep, they only respond to the voice of their shepherd. I like that. How like God to refer to us as His sheep desiring that we listen only to Him. If we, like sheep, will listen for and follow the voice of our Shepherd, we will possess a trust that leads to contentment.

Our world is changing at warp speed, with things occurring in the news each day that I never envisioned happening. The deceiver uses this to frighten me, and fear like all other temptation is sin to distract me. It is only when I listen for and follow God's voice that I am not afraid or alarmed. For me, no matter what is happening, underneath fear or questions, is the comfort that God gave His baby boy for me.

I repeat this in the books I write because God's actions speak His love to us. God gave me His best when I was at my worst. I can't get away from that. It gives me the courage to stay in the fight to trust in His character of courageous love. I am therefore content in the fact that I am here with great purpose *at this very time*, and so are you.

Elisabeth Elliot put it this way: "We ask, 'God, will it always be this way?' His reply, 'It's none of your business. My business is tomorrow. Your business is today. Do you love me? Then feed my lambs.'" I think Elisabeth was telling me to take my *yes face* and love the one in front of me—today.

"Lord, I want to be content. And I want to be more content at home than anywhere for that face in front of me. I want to learn contentment when I am pulled in a million directions. But how, Lord, can I be content? How with all these concerns racing through my mind can I really be there? This is hard, Lord. I'm scared. I'm discouraged, tired, and overwhelmed. Lord, please help me trust You with my days."

Learning the Secret

1. The if's and when's camping in our thoughts rob us of contentment. If I could lose this weight ~ when we make enough money ~ when we buy the right house ~ if I could find another job ~ when I make this next deal ~ if my kids would . . . ~ when I get a husband ~ if this had not happened in my life ~ if my husband would change ~ if I didn't have this husband ~ when I get it all together ~ if my family would get along ~ if she would just ~ when I have a baby ~ if I didn't have these kids ~ when I obtain justice....

   The list of '*discontentments*' goes on.

   Ok, the first digging deep question is: Am I typically content or discontent?

   _____

   _____

2. Let's think about some "ifs" and "whens" that creep into our thoughts and influence our attitudes, actions, and reactions. What do these thoughts look like for you? On a typical day what are some of your consuming thoughts?

   _____

   _____

3. We often feel we should know everything right now. But we don't! We can't! That's OK! Resting in the fact that we will be

in a learning curve for the rest of our lives makes each day a lot easier. This humble realization opens the door for us to learn the next thing. We learn, we fall, and we get up and learn more.

We are pursuing a lifetime contented in Christ, and a lifetime is made up of one day at a time. Have we perhaps walked through too many of our days with a knot in our stomach thinking we have to have everything figured out right now? What does that look like for you?

_____

_____

4. Is it easy for you to love the face in front of you and for you to really be wherever you are?

   Why or Why not?

_____

_____

5. Whoever I am at home is who I am! The rubber meets the road in my relationships at home and in the way I treat people in my world every day. How do I handle stress when my kids don't cooperate, when I receive lousy service, or when I am in a hurry? Is my contentment in Christ important to my family and my witness to my world?

_____

_____

6. Look at Philippians 4:4-6 for God's prescription to a peace that passes all understanding. What leads us to that peace?

_____

_____

7. According to Philippians 4:7 what guards our hearts and minds?

_____

_____

8. Write out Philippians 4:8, 9. Circle what we are to think on.

_____

_____

Paul's prescription for peaceful contentment is to be joyful and gentle, not to worry, and to be thankful and prayerful. It sounds impossible. It's possible, but supernatural. Right after Paul says "let your gentleness be evident to all," he says, "God is near." Yes, Jesus the Shepherd is right in the middle of our business. He is in us. He is with us. He sees every tear and knows our anxious hearts.

9. How do we get to that "contented trust" Paul learned when we are so much like Eve? Write out Philippians 4:12, 13.

_____

_____

Satan cannot have our salvation. He therefore seeks to rob us of our joy and contentment in Christ so we'll be a lousy witness to our world. May we learn through these pages to rest in that supernatural peace. May others wonder at the peace and contentment they see in us. Through these pages may we understand the war within us that keeps contentment just beyond our grasp, and learn the *secret* of following our Shepherd to the powerful peace and contentment He left us.

My days are His. He loves me deeply. As I allow the Holy Spirit to renew my mind, I will find contentment in His love. Like Paul, I choose *through His mighty power* to say, "What You have given me today, Lord, is enough. Your grace is amazing and You are enough."

2

My Seasons—All His

"This is the day the Lord has made. I will rejoice and be glad in it." He made it with eternal purpose. I am very glad about that, yet what *was* I thinking, writing about contentment? God wants me to believe what I'm writing—living and relating to it. It seems that as I begin another Bible study He is providing living color illustrations that I couldn't dream up if I tried. The last few weeks my Shepherd has watched me closely to see if I'm following Him, listening for His voice, and being content with where He's leading me.

That brings me to tonight. Tonight we buried my cat, Rowdy. Rowdy is not all the Lord has been gently prying from my tight clinched fingers though: stuff and status I thought I *needed* to be content. Don was at home for a school holiday. We had been doing things around the house, eating homemade enchiladas, praying together, taking a walk in the cold air, and watching on line a pair of eagles caring for their young. We also watched a 1930's John Wayne movie. It was a sweet day with my sweetheart. About five in the afternoon the phone rang. It was our son, Trent.

He said, "Momma, are you sitting down?"

"Yes," I said as I sat down.

This is the son who was a combat officer in the Marine Corps whom I have prayed through three wartime deployments as well as many other harrowing life events. I thought, *what in the world could have happened now?*

"Rowdy just died, Momma. He jumped up to his food bowl, let out a yowl, and died."

Rowdy had recently become Trent's cat. Though he was not lovable much of the time, thus the name Rowdy, he loved Don and me. He loved Don's mother—never laid a claw on her and slept on her feet when she came for a visit. He loved our grandson, Brave, who forgave him for his scratches and bites and affectionately called him Moon Cover. He also loved Trent who was not so forgiving, and being the recipient of one of Rowdy's infamous bites, chased him down the stairs with a broom.

Downsizing in a Supersize World

Less than two months before this day we had moved from a sleepy country town to an apartment in the city twenty minutes away. I said goodbye to the little red house, a lot of my 'stuff,' my beloved neighbors, mother's plants, the wild turkey, fox, and buzzard families, my old friends Margaret and Marie, my new friend Nancy, *and* my cat.

We had talked about the need to move closer to Don's work for a couple of years, but I had put it out of my mind. It came up off and on, and one weekend at a family wedding Don asked our sons to pray for us about God's will in the timing of a move. Never ask anyone to pray for you unless you expect them to and for God to answer. Two weeks later our plans to downsize, get off the concrete floors and stairs, eliminate house maintenance, and move closer to Don's work were in place. We had leased an apartment and planned to move the next month.

I shed some tears. I couldn't bear to tell my neighbors. I shed a few more tears. *It will make the grandkids so sad.* Then I began the task of dividing and conquering our 'stuff'. I kept what would fit in the apartment and the things I loved. I found new homes for the rest.

The task seemed daunting. Through it, I realized this move was not just about Don's commute and the stairs. The Lord wanted me to unload some of the things that took time away from what He was calling me to. He wanted me to simplify so I could focus more on His plan instead of mine. I knew that. As I worked though, my concern became Rowdy.

I hadn't wanted a cat. I had put my last old puppy dogs to sleep seven years before and decided I was not going to say good bye to another animal. That is until Rowdy, a wayward cat that belonged at the top of the hill, sat in the driveway for weeks looking sad and hungry. He wouldn't go home because he didn't like the competition the other cats and dogs presented at his house. Evening after evening I would pull into the driveway and see Rowdy sitting and waiting. I told Don we either had to move or I was going to buy cat food and feed that cat. I fed the cat.

"Lord," I said, "I know he's just a cat. But, would you help me with Rowdy? He is one of Your creatures. You sent him to us so we would love and care for him. He will have nothing to do with a cat box, and would be miserable cooped up in an apartment. He's left gutted squirrels on my porch, snatched hummingbirds out of the air, and scratched and bitten the grandkids. But he's ours. I don't want him to be lost or afraid. Would you take care of Rowdy, Lord?" That was my prayer.

Weeks passed. Much was accomplished. Plants dug, stuff relocated, house cleaned, compost pile moved, and Rowdy was delivered to Trent's hundred-year-old house in the historic district of Dallas. Rowdy had a big yard, trees, a fence to climb, and a lumbering puppy named Crockett to both run from and to torment. It didn't take him long to decide he was staying. He had gotten to the place where he was affectionate even with the dog. Their paws touched when they lay on the floor together and he sat next to Trent on the couch like he had with me.

This day Rowdy snuggled in the warm house, nibbled his food, went outside for a few minutes, and trotted through the house with Trent and Crockett. Then he jumped onto his table to nibble his food for the tenth time that day, and right there, he fell over and died. When Don and I arrived, Trent had dug a hole to bury Rowdy under his favorite tree, and I said goodbye to another animal I loved.

However, God answered my prayer. Though Rowdy had slowed down considerably in the last few years, neither we nor the vet knew he was sick. God knew Rowdy was a sick boy though. Until that very day he was loved and cared for, and he bit the dust in his favorite place, his dinner bowl.

Today Don's commute is shorter. With no concrete floors and stairs, my knees no longer ache, and I am more organized than I've been in my life. As I peck away on the computer in my sunny kitchen, though I have left behind the little red house, a lot of stuff, and my precious neighbors, I am at peace. I am content that God has us right where He wants us. It hasn't always been easy to trust what the Lord is doing, but the longer I follow the Shepherd the easier it becomes. Psalm 91 describes it as a secret place. "He who dwells in the secret place of the Most High will abide in the shadow of The Almighty" (Psalm 91:1).

In His shadow.

I like that.

When we're close to the Shepherd His shadow shelters us from the sun and wind—from harm. Yet when we are that close, it's hard for us to see what's around the next curve. He sees down the road though. I have a sense of anticipation at what the Lord has in mind for us here as I see people passing every day who need to know of His deep love for them. Though there are no foxes or wild turkeys in the city, as I work and write I watch the creatures God sent to remind me of His wonders. I listen to the twittering of birds and doves cooing at the bird feeder, watch green lizards puffing out their red throats, and smile at the bunnies resting in the morning sun. I also have grand dogs, who, like my grandchildren, I can love, spoil, and send home.

It's all good.

Each time we moved when I was a child my beautiful mother would say, "Dana, no matter where we go, all we need is our family and a few of our things around us, and it will be home." She was right. Even the grandchildren agree. This is Grammy's house—only smaller.

Though I can be consumed with circumstances, it does not change the fact that for a child of God, every season of my life is about people and their souls. If I am listening, I can hear Him ask me now as He has in seasons before, "Am I enough, Dana? Can you trust me with this? Can you trust that I know where I am leading you?"

Yes, Lord.

Yes, I can.

Life Has Seasons

Seasons: ~ babe in the womb ~ infant~ child ~ teen ~ education ~ first job ~ accident~ single ~ newlywed ~ new baby ~ many babies ~ no baby ~ no job ~ chronic illness ~ sudden death of a loved one ~ lingering death of a loved one ~ new job ~ divorce ~ single parenting ~ remarriage ~ retirement ~ growing old ~ stepping over to the other side.

Such is life.

Look at the perspective of the writer of Ecclesiastes. Read through these verses slowly and deliberately. They take on great meaning for me when I read them carefully and then listen for the voice of the Shepherd.

There is a time for everything,
    and a season for every activity under the heavens:
a time to be born and a time to die,
    a time to plant and a time to uproot,
a time to kill and a time to heal,
    a time to tear down and a time to build,
a time to weep and a time to laugh,
    a time to mourn and a time to dance,
a time to scatter stones and a time to gather them,

a time to embrace and a time to refrain from embracing,
a time to search and a time to give up,
a time to keep and a time to throw away,
a time to tear and a time to mend,
a time to be silent and a time to speak,
a time to love and a time to hate,
a time for war and a time for peace."

Ecclesiastes 3:1-8

God ordains our times. He is not surprised at what is going on. Through seasons we deal with sin, ignorance, hurt, and our need for God as we learn to trust Him enough to be content where we are and to touch the lives around us.

Courage in Change

We can trust the seasons of the year, can't we? Spring is followed by summer, then fall, and finally winter. Every year. Likewise, God is faithful in the seasons of our lives. Each has unique design and purpose, a beginning and an end. In the middle of a difficult season, it may seem God isn't hearing us, that He is not listening to our plea. But He is. In a hard winter plants die back and trees go dormant only to burst forth in great beauty in the springtime. Like the tough seasons of life, our winter will eventually change into springtime.

There is indeed "a time to every purpose under Heaven." Few people are comfortable with change. Some are terrified of it. Because change scares us, we often get in God's way as He is steering us around those curves toward a new season. We love consistency and predictability, because it gives us a sense of security. But two things about change are sure: it is inevitable and is often times unpredictable.

Sometimes the inevitable change of seasons is good news. Sometimes it's bad news. The good news is we are turning a corner in life to new things. The bad news is the Lord just might be leading us into a scary place. There have been days in my life when I was afraid of change because of fear of failure or of what people would think. But fear of change can sidetrack my walk with Christ.

Might I fail at what I try? Yes. But I should try anyway! Fear of change. Fear of failure. I can't let fear stop me. To grow, I let go of where I am and turn the corner to the change that awaits me. Who cares what people think? I don't need to be a people pleaser. I need to strive to be a God pleaser. If my primary concern is what God thinks and I am trying to please Him with my words and thoughts, then I am pleasing the right people.

Faith in the Wait

Some seasons are sweet, some are sorrowful, some are downright scary. We want to move through these times as fast as we can. To say "don't fight the season you are in" is bold when you're in the middle of a frightening or sorrowful time. Only God gets us from today to tomorrow though. Only God can lead us around those curves ahead. Only God can give us grace for each day as we grow and learn to trust Him more.

We have gone through a few of those in between jobs and out of ideas seasons. During those times we realized how much God loves us. We learned to check for sin in the camp, listening for what God was teaching us. Through those times He forged humility in us as He dug out pride. We learned to summon the prayers of others, because we needed folks in the trenches with us. We learned that while waiting on Him we had to do *all we could* to find that next assignment. We learned that in spite of our efforts though, nothing was going to happen until God pushed the button. Finally, we learned to stop holding our breath and to wait on Him.

Just to the east of the little red house are two of the most beautiful oak trees. They are perhaps 150 years old. When I stepped out my back door early in the morning and saw the sun rising behind those great oaks it took my breath away.

I presume that sometime in the 1800s acorns fell to the ground. Perhaps one of the ancestors of the cute little squirrels who scampered through my yard buried them in preparation for winter. From their activity two oak trees grew. They grew through plenty, through drought, and through flood. Some years they struggled. Some years they flourished. A lot of history happened as they grew. Now they are magnificent. And what was the most important contributor to their size and beauty? It was time. The elements were significant, but time made them what they are. It is time— one day and one season at a time that grows us into oaks of faith.

Look at the characters, stories, and scenarios in the Bible. These stories are about people who had no idea what was going on much of the time and obediently waited for God to do His thing, *or* disobediently rushed ahead and reaped the consequences of their unwillingness to wait. Much of our walk with Christ is *waiting* for the Shepherd's lead.

Isaiah was perhaps the greatest of the prophets calling the people of Israel, Judah, and the surrounding nations to turn to God. But the longer he proclaimed the truth, the more unpopular he became. In order to learn to trust God to bring justice from injustice, he learned to wait on Him. "The Lord longs to be gracious to you. He rises to show you compassion. For the Lord is a God of justice. Blessed are all who wait for Him" (Isaiah 30:15-18).

There is no faith without waiting. Like the cry of the prophets, there are times when I pray for people who are in heartbreaking circumstances or when I run to Him with my own broken heart and wail.

Dana to God: "How long, Lord? How long?"

My Lord always hears my cry. He reminds me of His love and He encourages me.

God to Dana: "Wait for me, Dana. I AM working."

For strength to go on, we wait. Waiting, learning, and trusting is a mystery of God and is part of the secret God worked in Paul and is working in us through times of waiting. During those times of waiting Don's favorite verse became, "Be joyful always, pray continually, and give thanks in all things" (1 Thessalonians 5:16, 17). Waiting on God brought these words to life in his heart. We couldn't make a job appear in our timing, so we waited for God to push that button. It was then that He opened our eyes to the needs of the homeless, a need we had been too busy to be aware of before. God had us right where He wanted us loving the faces in front of us. Through this wait a contented joy and thankful heart grew in us.

*"Those who wait upon the Lord shall renew their
strength; they will rise up on wings as eagles"
(Isaiah 40:31).*

Model of Contentment

Paul was in the "I'm in prison for the message of the cross"
season of life, as are more and more Christians around the world
today. It was hard. His journey of obedience must have seemed
impossible at times as he went around one curve after another
staying in the Shepherd's shadow. Yet, with each step, Paul was
learning the secret to contentment that he eventually wrote about.

God led him through dark valleys, across rocky places, by
still waters, and to mountain tops. Paul learned that he could trust
where God was leading him even though he could not see ahead.
Because Paul followed the Lord's lead, he influenced millions,
planted churches throughout the Gentile world, loved, taught, and
wrote, and his inspired words encompass much of the New
Testament.

Paul knew his success or failure had nothing to do with
what others said about him. It had nothing to do with the lies the
deceiver paraded through his mind or even his circumstances. All
that mattered was who God said he was, and that God would get
him wherever he needed to be. He was abused, hated, and rejected.
That rejection and abuse landed him in Rome under house arrest.
There he had access to Caesar's household—one more mission
field. Perhaps though imprisoned, he was walking in the greatest
freedom of his life. He was content in that hopeless circumstance
because he trusted the One Who led him there. Trust and love of

the Savior Who leads us to contentment (even in tough times) is not just for apostles or martyrs. God wants to lead us there, as well.

Nothing is for Nothing

Nothing is for nothing. This is the Dana paraphrase for Romans 8:28, 29. I get fresh lessons on this truth all the time—that all things are working for my good as God is changing me to look more like Him, so that I will impact my world for Christ.

God started with us, and He will finish with us. Though I was unaware of it at the time, God has been steering me in the direction He intended from always . . . even as a *teenager*. When I was sixteen, I started my first real job selling lingerie at a clothing store down the street. To be more specific, I stood behind the lingerie counter from 6-9 p.m. on Thursday evenings. I didn't know a thing about selling underwear. I may have made two sales that spring. God didn't waste that experience on me though. From lingerie sales, I learned who I was not. I'm not a salesman. I can't sell anything but Jesus, and Jesus sells Himself.

When summer came I started a job as a server in a chicken restaurant across the parking lot from the clothing store. From serving chicken, I got a hint of who I am. The work was hard, and I did a lousy job for a while. It was not until the end of the summer that I learned to cut those lemons *quickly* for the iced tea and to get orders straight enough to serve the customers well.

Do you remember the *yes face* I learned from Teddy Roosevelt? Though I was unaware of it at the time on a Sunday afternoon when the church crowd came through, I observed some real *yes faces*. The restaurant was full, and my station included a table in the side room that was enormous. A family came in and filled the table. This precious family waited and waited as I blundered through their order and finally served them. In front of me the entire time sat a table of *yes faces* from daddy and mommy down to baby. This family had obviously been to church, loved Jesus, and poured out His love to me.

Each evening when my folks or brother, Tim, picked me up and I got in the car smelling like lemons and fried chicken, I had learned something. I learned that I love people, and I love serving them. God was leading me on a path even then. I didn't know I would have a large family, friends, brothers and sisters in Christ, and decades of children and women to love, teach, and serve. But God did. He was pointing me to today and has been taking me around those curves ever since.

Dear Lord, give us your amazing grace to live in contentment where we are, to have the courage and trust in You to move on when You say so, and to know that because of the cross nothing is for nothing. In Jesus beautiful name, Amen

Learning the Secret

1. Trusting God means we don't know what's going on much of the time. This is faith. How hard is it for us to trust God with what is out ahead of us? Write Hebrews 11:8. This verse shows what God showed Abraham about what was ahead.

   _____

   _____

   Abraham did not know where he was going. Yet God was getting Abraham and his family where they needed to be for His purpose. God is getting us to *a place for His purpose*, as well.

2. How often are we discontent in the season we are in—ever longing for the next? Look at the life of Moses. What was going on in his life during these seasons?

   Exodus 1:15-16

   Exodus 2:1-10

   Exodus 2:11-15

   Exodus 3:1

   Exodus 3:10

It's easy to look back and see that God was using each season of Moses' life to prepare him for the next. His ultimate purpose as an eighty-year-old man was to set the nation of Israel free from 400 years of bondage. Yet forty years earlier he left Egypt a total failure. He was a murderer, disgraced in the eyes of the Egyptians and unable to do one thing to help his own people. After crossing the desert, he spent the next forty years tending sheep. God was not through with him though. These forty years were quite a demotion from prince of Egypt to shepherd in the wilderness, but it was God's final preparation (humbling and strengthening him) for the job to come. Failure is humiliating, but it's an effective way for God to teach us new things and is often the way He moves us where He wants us to be.

I can relate. I have loved to teach school since I graduated from college. Like being a wife and mother, I loved being a teacher. It was a great part of my identity. There was a time though, where the circumstances in which I found myself made me *feel* like I had never been a good teacher and never could be. I felt like a failure, and a sense of failure kicks the wind out of us. It's painful. But God is there. He's not made a mistake. Just as with Moses, He uses humiliating circumstances to take us around those curves to that next place. Humility is that important element that has taught me total dependency on God.

3. What are the things you enjoy and that give you comfort and a sense of safety?

_____

_____

4. Of these securities, is there anything you have had to let go of along the way?

_____

_____

5. You may be in a peaceful season of life. Or you may be in a tough season. Are you aching to get past this place? If that is the case, what do you hope to escape?

_____

_____

6. How has fear stopped you from making needed changes, moving forward, and doing some things you are pretty sure God wants you to do?

_____

_____

7. Look back in the chapter at Ecclesiastes 3:1-8. Think about insight you might have gleaned from these verses which

give you a sense of peace as you seek to believe that there is a time to every purpose under heaven.

_____

_____

8. Write out Romans 8:28, 29 and circle the words *all, for good, loved, called, conformed to the image of God.*

_____

_____

Wow! Could God be more emphatic? These beautiful yet mysterious words are true.

I cry out to God for the grace to trust Him instead of kicking my way through my days and the season in which He has me. It is then that I begin to bloom where I'm planted. Our world longs for real-deal-followers of Christ who trust God and live like it. Graciously failing is evidence of one of those real deal folks. It doesn't mean they don't hurt or are not afraid. It just means they are learning to trust God through the hurt and fear. I continue to learn more about "failing with grace" and being content with what God has provided. It gives me the courage to move to a new place even though it's frightening.

Dana to God: "I trust you, Lord. It's hard! It hurts. It's humiliating. I'm scared! But, Lord, You're with me. You've got this thing. Teach me, Lord, to trust You more." The father who wanted Jesus to cast evil spirits out of his son declared, "I do believe; help my unbelief" (Mark 9:24). When the disciples who had not been able to cast out these demons asked Jesus why they couldn't, "He replied, this kind can only come out by prayer" (Mark 9:29).

When we fight our battles alone, we are filled with stress and fear. We can't fight these battles with our *want to*. The battle is the Lord's and has to be fought by prayer and through the Holy Spirit. We fight with spiritual weapons to win the war for a heart of contentment. We fight with spiritual weapons for the powerful life it displays. This is where the battle is fought and won. We'll learn more about the spiritual fight in the chapters to come. But we start here learning to pray God's word with a few scriptures and to get to know God through His word.

Our faith in Who He is and the depth of His love for us grows through His word and by His Spirit. So does love, joy, peace, and purpose. These are the fruit of a heart of contentment. The enemy of God hates it when we realize where the battle is as we begin to hide the word of God in our hearts.

So let's do it!

There are many ways to meditate upon and get the word of God into our hearts. Some of you can easily memorize scripture by reading or saying the verses. You might not need help at all, but memorizing is difficult for me. I use this method that I learned from my daughter-in-love, Kristi, who has hidden much of God's word in her heart.

I write the scripture at the top of my prayer journal page. Then, I write the first letter of each word in vertical columns going down the page. I read the scripture through numerous times. Each day I run my finger down the vertical columns while saying the scripture a few times, and it's not long until I have it. Each bit of the word of God in me is a bit more of God in me. It makes me more fit for the battle waging against me for my peace and contentment.

Whether you use this method or not, I encourage you to let God renew your heart and mind by filling it with His words, because knowing His word is the path to intimacy with Jesus and the way to peace. You might not need vertical letters to learn scripture though. You may read them and know them. You may sing scripture to learn them or speak the word right out loud. That's powerful! It is the very bread of life, so whatever you do, begin to read His words.

Lord, give me a hunger for your words and help me to hide them in my heart in Jesus' name. Amen

---

"Set your mind on things above" Colossians 3:2

To set something down we have to be intentional. Set is an action word! My mind will not go God's way unless I set it there.

S
Y
M
O
T
A.   Colossians 3:2

"The mind governed by the Spirit is life and peace" (Romans 8:6b).

T   I

M   L

G   A

B   P. Romans 8:6

T

S

"May these words of my mouth and this meditation of my heart be pleasing in your sight, Lord, my Rock and my Redeemer" (Psalm 19:14).

M   B

T   P

W   I

O   Y

M   S

M   L

A   M

T   R

M   A

O   M

M   R. Psalm 19:14

H

3

My Perspective, My Possessions, My People. They Are All His

"Everything in heaven and earth is Yours, oh Lord, and this is Your kingdom"
1 Chronicles 29:11

Most unhappy people, whatever they think they are unhappy about, have one thing in common: They are discontented. The dictionary meaning for discontentment is: a restless longing, prolonged unfulfilled desire and a longing for something other than the present situation. Much discontentment in life is a result of comparing ourselves to others and to what they have. They have more stuff or make more money. Their home is more beautiful or their husband got the promotion. Their kids are healthier, made the team, or got the lead in the play.

The secret that Paul embraced which gave him such peace is the knowledge and acceptance that everything is God's. Everything belongs to Him. It doesn't matter what that kid's last name is or the name on the mortgage or check stub; everything in heaven and earth has been given to us to care for—but belongs to God. Living in light of that knowledge is a perspective changer.

Perspective of *Get-To*, Not *Got-To*

I love to use Don for illustrations, and he is a good sport for allowing me to. He is a love, but he is also a recovering obsessive compulsive perfectionist. In his younger years, his default was being too hard on himself and anyone else in the world who was out of line. He could never relax. He got up each day dutifully saying, "I have to do this. I have to do that."

It wore me out.

I am a go getter. I perfected that skill when I was a single parent. But my default is slow and easy. I need recovery time to be the best I can be. Eventually, my reply to Don's "We have to" was, "We *don't* have to do it, honey. We *get* to do it. If we were dead or alone we wouldn't have to do any of this. Because we are breathing, have family, a job, a pet, a house, a friend, a purpose, a Savior, we *get* to do a lot of things!"

I decide each day if I am going to do my doing with a "got-to" or "get-to" attitude. A get-to attitude is simply being thankful for what God had given us. That thankful heart is the difference between an ulcer and a good night's sleep.

Our perspective of truth is truth to us. So if our default is OCD or we've been the recipient of a lot of criticism in our life, we are going to have to work harder to let go and trust God enough to be content. But each day is a gift, life is seasons, and God is in the middle of it. Therefore, if I am growing in the image of God day by day, a get-to God perspective of life is growing in me.

Right? My heart should be changing as I read God's love letter, listen for His voice, and follow Him. Right?

Yes and no. Sometimes my attitude slips back into that dutiful default. A number of years ago my doctor told me to walk, to walk for my heart, for my back and knees, and for my joy. I have endeavored to do that, and long ago these walks turned into prayer walks which I love. For a long time though, my perspective was wrong. The praying part I loved. The getting out and walking part I didn't relish because I had to stop what I was doing! I don't know how many times I told Don, "I *have* to walk today!"

While walking through the mountains in Colorado under a glorious sky one summer morning God so gently administered to my heart an attitude check *and* an adjustment. I marveled at the breathtaking beauty and basked in the sweet breeze and sunshine on my face. The colors, the sounds, the smells, the textures, the animals, the water, and the sky were all glorious.

In the midst of that sensory delight I was convicted of my stinkin' attitude.

Dana to God: Have to walk? What if I couldn't walk, Lord?

God to Dana: "Each step is a gift, Dana."

Dana to God: "As usual, You are right Lord. I don't have to walk. *I get to walk.*"

I laughed out loud. God was giving me the get-to talk that Don receives from me. Attitude adjusted. If God is the sovereign God who loves me with an incomparable love, and if every appointment is a divine appointment, then I don't have to do anything. I don't even have to obey.

I get to!

Perspective of Gratitude

One afternoon long ago, I had an encounter with a *have to* momma in the grocery store. She and her husband were good evangelical folks with a house full of kids that they homeschooled. I looked to this older Christian woman for some encouragement in the Lord, but the conversation had hardly begun before she began to gripe about her husband and her pitiful life.

At the time, I was a working mother and raising my sons alone. I mowed, cooked, cleaned, sewed, and prayed—looking for the energy to walk through each day. It hurt my heart that she was so ungrateful for what God had given her: a husband who worked hard for her family and the opportunity to school her kids at home. I am sure she did not realize that I was looking for a flicker of the light of Jesus in her. Yet, this gal looked like she had taken a bite out of a dill pickle and her pickle-suckin' attitude of ingratitude saddened me.

In Texas we call this griping. I used to tell my sons and students, "Remember what happened to the Hebrews. They were gripers. God has no patience with griping, and they died in the desert." We can't gripe about everything and find contentment. Ingratitude will overtake and consume our search for contentment every time. Likewise, if we take in too much of the culture, we'll be griping about our pitiful life like so many characters in sitcoms and movies. This is deadly serious for a believer in Jesus Christ. It's fodder for the devil.

The Hebrew's griping landed them a forty-year stint in the desert where all but Joshua and Caleb died. These two men were faced with the same fears and circumstances as those around them, but they chose to believe God. They had a get-to attitude. No doubt their circumstances were scary and beyond difficult. No doubt some of your circumstances are, as well. But these two men of God chose to trust Him in the midst of scary and difficult circumstances. God took notice of them, and forty years later they were the only two of that generation who entered the Promised Land.

Thankful for each step
Each breath
Food for the day
A morning and an evening
A child, a brother, a grandchild, a friend, a neighbor
The cross
Thankful

Perspective of Right or Wrong vs. Right or Left

Confusing right and wrong with right and left will rob us of contentment as well. God's standard determines right and wrong. If God says it's right, it's right. If God says it's wrong, it's wrong. Often though, we agonize over decisions that are right or left—not moral standards but decisions that have to do with our preference or need.

Some of us replace the toilet paper to pull from the top, some from the bottom. Some of us scalp our yards in the spring.

Some do not. Some like a high and tight hair cut. Some like it bushy, straight, or curly.

We put importance in different things. We raise our kids differently and choose the kind of education they receive. We drink skim, 2%, or whole milk. We choose to travel or not to. Some work outside the home. Some do not. We live wherever need or desire dictates. These right or left decisions fill our days. Until I began to understand this, the right and lefts often gave me a nervous stomach.

In these right and lefts, I eventually learned a few things. I learned that if I don't like the way things are going, or if God shows me something new, I simply turn and go another way. I learned that I should give others grace in this area too. Just because they don't do things the way I would, I don't need to judge that they are doing them wrong. My step-daughters, daughters-in-law, sisters-in-law, and friends have different ways of doing things in the way we cook, clean, raise kids, communicate with our husbands, and replace the toilet paper. It's all good!

Right or wrong. These are moral absolutes exemplified by Christ and proclaimed in the word of God. "I, the Lord, speak the truth. I declare what is right" (Isaiah 45:19).

Right or left. Give the people in your life a break—including yourself. Do what you prefer or have need for, and if you learn something new or change your mind, change direction.

Perspective of Fair

Speaking of perspective, we often miss the fact that fair is not always even. We children of the King most certainly try the best we can to show fairness. Proverbs 1:3 tells us to do what is just, right, and fair. We expect others to be fair with us, as well. Yet in this fallen world life will inevitably produce circumstances for us and our families that are not fair. If we are waiting for the world to be fair before we are content, we will wait a lifetime.

How many times do we hear people say, "This isn't fair!"? How many times have we said it or thought it ourselves? The world in which we live is becoming increasingly an entitlement society with folks who think it is OK in every circumstance to stomp their feet and shout "That's not fair!" This is not an unfamiliar response. It goes back a long way. That's what Lucifer and Eve did. Remember? The fact is though; fair is not always even.

This was the case in our house when I was growing up. I was the only child—the last hatch in the nest of five children— whose college was paid for. Because I was the child my parents could afford to help through school, they did. My beloved older siblings worked or served in the military paying for their own college education. Yet I never once heard them mention that my college was paid for and theirs was not. I am very thankful for my brothers and sister. Like my mother who found herself in unfair circumstances much of her life, I never heard from them, "This isn't fair." Fair is not always even in God's economy either.

Satan authored the concept that fair has to be even, and gullible Eve followed. Yet if fair were even we would all have the same gifts, trials, children, spouses, jobs, paychecks, relationship problems, climate, ears, and noses. All we have to do is look at the cross to see that fair is not even. It was not fair for Christ to die for me when I was at my worst. He shouldn't have gone to the cross for me.

It's not fair.

But it is just.

If fair were always even, we would die without Christ paying for our sin. In God's justice and love though, Christ paid what we owed. "God demonstrates His own love for us in this: While we were still sinners, Christ died for us" (Romans 5:8). Sometimes our todays are unfair, yet we serve a God of perfect justice who loves us deeply. Our God, our Shepherd, can and does use 'unfair' for our good and to His glory.

My Possessions

Perhaps I need to ask myself, "Do I own my stuff or does my stuff own me?" To help us answer this question let's look at the story of the rich young ruler in the book of Matthew. "Teacher, what good thing shall I do that I may obtain eternal life?" And He said to him, "Why are you asking Me about what is good? There is *only* One who is good; but if you wish to enter into life, keep the commandments." *Then* he said to Him, "Which ones?" And Jesus said, "You shall not commit murder; You shall not commit adultery; You shall not steal; You shall not bear false witness; Honor your father and mother; and You shall love your neighbor as yourself." The young man said to Him, "All these things I have kept; what am I still lacking?" Jesus said to him, "If you wish to be complete, go *and* sell your possessions and give to *the* poor, and you will have treasure in heaven; and come, follow Me."

But when the young man heard this statement, he went away grieving; for he was one who owned much property. And Jesus said to His disciples, "Truly I say to you, it is hard for a rich man to enter the kingdom of heaven. Again I say to you, it is easier for a camel to go through the eye of a needle, than for a rich man to enter the kingdom of God." When the disciples heard *this*, they were very astonished and said, "Then who can be saved?" And looking at *them* Jesus said to them, "With people this is impossible, but with God all things are possible" (Matthew 19:16-26 NASB).

The rich young ruler had kept the commandments Jesus asked of him. He was a good guy. But he didn't own his possessions, **they owned him.** When Jesus asked him if he could forgo his comforts and give to the poor, he sadly realized he could not. The rich young ruler's stuff, bank account, and plans for it, owned him. He was consumed with materialism.

Materialism. We live in the midst of great blessing in our country. Yet our greatest blessings can become our greatest snares. Because materialism is an attitude of the heart not the size of our bank account, it snares both the rich and poor. Millions of dollars are made in the storage business each year in the U.S., because we accumulate and store a *lot* of stuff. We fill our homes with stuff, then our garages. Then we build bigger homes and fill them. Even though the chief cause of conflict in marriage in America is financial issues, we keep filling up those storage buildings.

Interestingly, the word materialism translates to worry or a divided mind. Though we feel protected by our stuff, it causes us to worry. If we don't have much, we worry about getting more. If we have a lot, we worry about keeping what we have. Too much stuff can complicate my life. In the recesses of my muddled brain is a burden about my excess stuff. The stuff that needs to be organized, cleaned, fixed, and finished. I'm talking about *excess* here. My excess causes me to be double minded and can rob me of contentment. Like the rich young ruler, if my stuff owns me, whether I have a lot or whether I have a little, it will make me discontent.

Often in marriage one spouse is a spender and one is a saver, or one puts value in one thing, and one another. This was certainly the case for Don and me. For years I misunderstood Don reserving money so we could go to Colorado each summer. I thought we should use that money the other 11½ months of the year on *stuff*. I love to nest! I want to provide a God glorifying place with safe, peaceful, and pretty surroundings for friends and family to gather.

This was my thinking. *So we are going to scrimp during the year to drive seventeen hours to CO, exacerbating my sciatica, to live in a tent, and work our tails off, so we can start each school year exhausted*

I thought he was so selfish.

Eventually though, I realized that my man needed this. He has loved to dry fly fish in the streams in Colorado since his grandfather taught him as a little boy, and he is good at it. He catches fish when no one else can. Because he is a sanctified perfectionist, he pushes himself to do things well and thoroughly all the time. The best way therefore, for him to recharge and be ready to work hard for another year is to drive seventeen hours, sleep in a tent, and spend a few days in the river.

Yes, God has put a desire to nest in women's hearts, and it's good. When momma birds nest they gather twigs and leaves. When we nest though, we gather stuff. So I must ask myself, "How much is enough, Dana?" Aware that materialism will make me double minded, I must ask at times, "How much is enough?"

Some of us have closets and drawers full of clothes that we might wear *someday*. Or we store boxes in the attic for *someday*. In becoming acquainted with people who live on the streets and with those who work with them I have learned about things I might need someday. I have learned that they need many things *today*. Ministries and organizations that meet the needs of the poor are in need *today* of the things we might just need someday.

I promise you, it will give you great pleasure to let go of some of your stuff. It has eased my heart to simply give, and as a result to get those drawers and closets cleaned out. After all, "Everything in heaven and earth is Yours, O Lord, and this is Your kingdom" (2 Chron. 29:11). Taking my stuff off the idol list by letting some of it go, and being thankful for what I have instead of pining for what I don't have, releases my heart to be single mindedly content in Him.

My People—We're Different: God Made Us That Way

If he would . . .

If she would . . .

If they would . . .

It started in the garden. The man said, "The woman you put here with me—she gave me some fruit from the tree, and I ate it" (Genesis 3:12). *People! It's these people you gave me that are the problem, Lord. They aren't like me!* Hmmm . . . Is it the people in our lives who are the problem, or is it the way we respond to them?

My oldest son, Chris was methodical and introspective. He loved reading and learning. He had gentle eyes, a sweet smile, and at three had the vocabulary of a college professor. He popped out of the womb inquisitive, kind, and cautious. As the Lord taught me things, I taught Chris, and he ate it up.

Parker, my number two son, hit the floor laughing and looking for adventure. He was filled with joy—a smile from ear to ear and a twinkle in his eye. He climbed on everything he could find. One summer afternoon he found a wooden fence. He climbed up, and he slid down. He let out a yowl that drew neighbors from every direction. While he and I cried, my sweet neighbors extracted ten or so large splinters from his tummy and legs.

A few weeks later I found Parker under the kitchen table peering up at me with his twinkling eyes. He had just consumed a bottle of baby aspirin. That twinkle vanished when I forced him to swallow medicine that made him throw up his toe nails. That night everyone was finally sleeping and all was quiet in the house.

Dana to God: "Lord, what am I going to do with this kid?

God to Dana: "He's the way I made him. Love him, guide him, and train him. It will take a few more spankings with this one to keep him from killing himself. But you wouldn't want them the same, would you?"

Dana to God: No, I wouldn't.

I just *thought* Parker was full of adventure! When Trent came along, his spirit of adventure trumped Parker's considerably. He was the designated crash dummy for any idea the brothers came up with always coming up exclaiming, "Do it again!" When he started talking, he talked *all* the time. So much so that Chris would beg, "Momma, please make him stop!"

Case in point—we are all different. We know that, yet we often <u>misunderstand and judge</u> these differences as wrong. We can disapprove of both the big *and* little people around us because they are not like us. My wanting to create the people around me into my image though, is getting into God's business. We're not talking about sin patterns here, but differences. God has not made any mistakes in the temperaments, personalities, bents, gifts, and struggles He has given us, our kids, or others. No mistakes. Yet we make comparisons and can become judgmental, envious, or jealous.

Cain was jealous of Abel. Saul was jealous of David. The Pharisees were jealous of Jesus. And Peter was jealous of John. Peter's jealousy was more subtle though. After the resurrection as Jesus and his disciples were walking along the road, Jesus challenged Peter's commitment to Him. Knowing that Peter had denied Him three times the night He was betrayed, Jesus asked him three different times if he loved Him. Then He told Peter how he would suffer and die for Him. Ouch! Peter then looked back at John who was following behind them and asked Jesus, "What about him?"

Jesus' simple reply was, "He's not your business. Follow me." That is good advice from the Master for Peter *and* for us. Many things concerning others that get in our knickers are not our business. Perhaps we need to reconsider our benevolent involvement in the problems of extended family, or with grown children, neighbors, or friends. Perhaps we are even micromanaging our little people too much—instead of praying.

Though it was none of Peter's business, we know God had a great plan for John. For the sake of the cross he was exiled to the Isle of Patmos. While he was exiled on that island though, he was inspired by the Holy Spirit to write the last book of the Bible, The Revelation. It is both the end and beginning of the story of God and man. John's future was not Peter's business. It was God's business.

Between Them and God—Between Me and God

I'm lying in bed thinking about people I love who are hurting. *Will it ever be better, Lord? Will there ever be peace? Help them, Lord, help them.* No doubt God passes the names of folks through my mind so I will pray for them. I do pray, but those thoughts can pretty quickly turn to worry.

Dana to God: Lord, this is worry, isn't it?

God to Dana: Yes, but I'm right here, Dana. Look at me. Listen for me. Pray for them, and leave them to Me.

Dana to God: I've been listening to the voice of the stranger, haven't I, Lord? I know You love them much more than I do. Help that to sink deep in my soul. You love me and any soul I am burdened to pray for much more than I do. You have a purpose for all of us. Oh Lord, if I didn't absolutely know that You love us more than we can imagine and nothing we do will change that, my heart would break over the broken hearts in the world around me. So I place them once again under Your love—right at the foot of the cross.

I Can't Fix Them – I'm Not Supposed To

Most of us want peace around us, yet we live in a world filled with offences. Yes, our family, friends, and co-workers are a bunch of sinners just like we are. So how do we deal with the drama queens and kings in our life? Are we drawn into their drama? The devil wants us to be. What about neighbors? Most neighbors are friendly enough once they know you're not an ax murderer. But I have had a few neighbors who, when I give them a friendly greeting, act like they are part of a witness protection program. Maybe they are! They look at me like, "Lady, you talkin' to me?" That used to bother me greatly. I wanted everyone to be happy, and their bad attitude or mood would jump right on me.

It took me a long time to learn not to allow other people's confusion, moods, or ill temper to affect me. Most times people carry burdens of which I know nothing. So whether they respond to my chipper greeting or not there is one thing I can do for them. I can control my response and my attitude, and I can pray. Unless I am marooned on a desert island or in solitary confinement, God is going to use *people* to sanctify me as He conforms me into His image.

Though it is tough to pray for people who are hard to get along with, rude or mean, that is where the battle is. The most powerful thing we can do for every person in our world is pray for them. Talk less and pray more. Ultimately it's between me and God. It's between them and God. I have counseled numerous women who have family members who have spent a lifetime manipulating others. Then they wait for them to predictably react to them.

My counsel to them: recognize the pattern and determine to no longer react, to no longer let this 'thing' jump on them, to no longer answer the door when the devil knocks.

At some point, the Lord convicted me that just like Peter with John; when I react to other's sin, I'm trying to do God's job.

When I let others' lousy attitude become my lousy attitude, then I became the one sinning.

I can't control others. I can't fix them. I'm not supposed to.

God is, so I keep my eye on the Shepherd.

And I pray.

For some perspective: the pastors in the Middle East urge us to pray not for them, but for their persecutors. The persecuted church understands why we are here. They see the bigger picture - the souls of men. When we think of people who make our stomach churn, we need to ask ourselves, "Who is praying for them?" "Is anyone praying for them?" Though healthy boundaries may be necessary with hard people, we should pray for them *and* be patient. Instead of letting them get under our skin, we can turn our thoughts of them to prayer.

Christ's last prayer before He was taken to the cross was for us—for unity in the body of Christ. He prayed that we would be one as He and His Father are one. Therefore, when there is a breach between us and others we should try to open the door for reconciliation. We forgive and let it go. If they receive our offer of reconciliation—good. If they don't, it's not our problem. Keep praying for them and remember ultimately it's between you and God. It's between them and God. Leave it to the Shepherd.

Contentment is not in location, vocation, position, possessions, or people.

It's in a condition.

The condition is loved.

We are loved.

Learning the Secret

1. Read Genesis 16 about Hagar, and Genesis 37:23-28 about Joseph. What do these two Biblical characters have in common?

    _____

    _____

2. Was God, the Shepherd, leading both Hagar and Joseph even in their utter despair? What was up ahead for them?

    _____

    _____

3. Read Matthew 19:16-26

    a. What verse becomes a snare to the rich young ruler?

    _____

    _____

    b. Verse 22 shows us that the rich young ruler was troubled by his own decision. What do you think motivated him *not* to accept Jesus' offer to follow Him? (one word)

_____

_____

c. In verses 23 and 24 Jesus states that it is hard for a rich man
    to enter the kingdom of God. Why so?

_____

_____

d. Is it possible for us to be very wealthy, yet not
    materialistic? (verse 26)

_____

_____

e. Do I own my stuff or does my stuff own me? Do I have a
    problem with materialism?

_____

_____

4. Do you now have or have you had a difficult person/people in
    your life. What has that looked like?

_____

_____

How are you handling that relationship?

_____

_____

5. In John 14:27 what did Christ leave us?

_____

_____

6. What was Christ's last prayer for his disciples and for us in John 17:20-23?

_____

_____

Peace and unity. Jesus left us peace and prayed for us to live in unity.

The only path to that peace is staying within earshot of the Shepherd's voice. There is no other way. When I can't sleep I get to practice what I preach. I lay there warm, comfortable *and* wide awake. I begin to speak God's sweet words in my mind (so I won't wake up Don.) The beauty of knowing His word is that I can let those sweet words pour through and over me. They are prayer for all that concerns me knowing that "He whose mind is stayed on Thee has perfect peace."

Perfect Peace. Thank you, Lord.

Romans 12:1,2 "Therefore I urge you brothers and sisters in view of God's mercy, to offer your bodies as a living sacrifice, holy and pleasing to God – this is your true and proper worship. Do not be conformed to the pattern of this world, but be transformed by the renewing of your mind. Then you will be able to test and approve what God's will is, His good, pleasing and perfect will."

T	L	C	T	P
I	S,	T	Y	A
U	H	T	W	P
Y	A	P	B	W
B	P	O	A	
A	T	T	T	
S	G -	W,	T	
I	T	B	A	
V	I	B	A	
O	Y	T	W	
G	T	B	G	
M,	A	T	W	
T	P	R	I,	
O	W.	O	H	
Y	D	Y	G	
B	N	M.	Romans 12:1,2	
A	B			

"I have been crucified with Christ and I no longer live but Christ lives in me. The life I now live in the body, I live by faith in the Son of God who loved me and gave His life for me" (Galatians 2:20).

I	L	T	T
H	I	L	S
B	M.	I	O
C		N,	G,
W		L	W
C		I	L
A		T	M
I		B,	A
N		I	G
L		L	H
L		B	F
B		F	M.
C		I	

Galatians 2:20

4

By His Spirit—All His

Who is going to help me know my Father and find contentment in Him? Who will enable me to love and obey Him so I will look more like Him every day? Who will give me perfect peace? Who will fight this battle for me? It is by the Spirit of the Living God. This fight is All His! Remember Peter denying Jesus three times in John 18, and then in John 21 Jesus asked Peter three times if he loved Him? Remember Peter looking back at John and asking, "What about him?" Peter's intentions were good. Jesus knew his heart. I'm sure he read God's word. He probably knew a lot of it, but he seemed helpless to line his thoughts and actions up with God's truth—just like us.

Yet the next time we see Peter in Acts 2, he is a different man. Jesus changed Simon's name to Peter which translated Petros or the rock. God's word was brought to life in him, and he preached and taught the message of the cross first to hundreds and then to thousands. Peter became the rock upon which Christ would ultimately build His church. How did Peter get from John 18 to Acts Chapter 2?

The disciples had spent forty days with Jesus after the resurrection. As they watched Him ascend into heaven, they probably had a boatload of unanswered questions. But this time instead of bolting, they did what He told them to do. Though they were hunted men, they stayed in Jerusalem and they waited. For ten days, they waited and prayed. On the tenth day something amazing happened which changed them.

"When the day of Pentecost came, they were together in one place. Suddenly a sound like the blowing of a violent wind came from heaven and filled the whole house where they were sitting. They saw what seemed to be tongues of fire that separated and came to rest on each of them, and they were filled with the Holy Spirit and began to speak in other tongues as the Spirit enabled them (Acts 2:1-4). Then Acts 2:14 reads, "Then Peter stood up with the eleven, raised his voice and addressed the crowd: 'Fellow Jews and all of you who live in Jerusalem, let me explain this to you; listen carefully to what I say.'"

Fifty days had passed since that horrible night when the disciples had run away in fear and Peter had denied the Lord three times. Now he was preaching to a crowd of thousands. It was Pentecost and there were Jews in Jerusalem from all over the known world. Acts tells us they were Parthians, Medes, Elamites, residents of Mesopotamia, Judea, Cappadocia, Pontus, Asia, Phrygia and Pamphylia, Egypt, Libya, Cyrene, Rome, Crete and Arabia. Some of these visitors were claiming that the disciples were drunk that morning, because they could not explain hearing them speaking in their own languages any other way.

They weren't drunk though. They were filled with the Spirit of God. Fifty days earlier Peter would have been intimidated by this multicultural crowd of Jews, yet this day he stood boldly before them and led them to the King of the Jews, Jesus. What changed Peter from a fearful, jealous follower of Christ with good intentions into Petros—the Rock, a rockin' preacher of the gospel? The Helper, The Holy Spirit Jesus spoke of had come to them. The Holy Spirit transformed *Peter's* life first, then the lives of those around him. It moved the location of that knowledge and experience from his head to his heart. Through these men the Holy

Spirit exploded salt and light—the message of the cross — throughout the world.

They had prayed and waited on God, and on Pentecost God sent the third person of the Trinity to be their Helper. The word "helper" in Greek is *Paraclete*—which means to "come alongside." The Holy Spirit *comes alongside* us and consoles, comforts, encourages, uplifts, refreshes, intercedes, counsels, teaches, helps, and sets us free. Amen.

Jesus told the disciples before he left that because He would not be with them physically, he would send a Helper. Their Shepherd would keep leading them by His Holy Spirit. The Spirit leads us as well. God is the boss, and our Shepherd, but He is *first* our Father. God is our Daddy (Abba) first.

Our Daddy has given us the Holy Spirit. It is the Spirit of the Living God in us—the very Spirit that raised Jesus from the dead, parted the seas, and created all life in the universe. It is in the power of the Holy Spirit that we *get to*—not have to—obey, teach, preach, love, give kindness, live in unity, receive wisdom and discernment, and have joy and peace. It is also in His Spirit that we fight!

Paradise Really was Lost

If Christ sent His sweet Holy Spirit to abide in us, then what happened? Why is it so hard to obey, to trust, and to be content? Is it because paradise really was lost? Yes, paradise was lost. The world that is, is not the world that was. Paul knew that he was in a deadly war and was totally dependent on his Shepherd to guide him. Eve had no idea that discontentment in what her Father had given her would take her to a place of rebellion. In Eve we see our need to listen for the Shepherd's voice and follow Him.

Because, like Eve, the whisperings of the deceiver pull us away from God's voice, and our minds and hearts quickly wander to that place of discontent.

Jesus said, "My peace I leave you, my peace I give you." He left me peace through the Holy Spirit. I learned early in my walk with Christ though, that I would have to fight the lies of the stranger to possess God's gift of peace and contentment. Just as Joshua had to fight for the land already promised to God's people, we must be engaged in the spiritual fight to possess peace. This war can't be won in our flesh. Eve's battle is our battle.

Her thoughts might have gone a little like this:

Working with the fragrance of jasmine and lavender lingering in the air is pure delight. The gentle breeze brushes against my face and the sunshine warms my back. We are surrounded by a symphony of fluttering wings and chirping as birds of every kind go about their work. They are as varied and vibrant in color and shape as the blooms spilling over hedges and bursting from the trees. Every green imaginable is beneath our feet and hangs overhead. Dainty flowers dance in the wind in deepest blues and purples and the purest of white. Above, the eagle's nest flutters with life. Below, sheep nibble sweet grass; a mamma nuzzles her lamb.

All this and more is in the garden my husband and I keep. It's Father's place. His love surrounds and fills us. After our work is done, we walk with Him. He talks. We listen. We talk. He listens.

In the companionship of my husband, I find safety and joy, and together we rest in the care of the One who loves us unconditionally. He has blessed us with life and peace. Yet one prohibition our Father has given.

Just one . . .

My mind is wandering away from Father's voice, but I believe it is alright for my thoughts to linger a bit longer.

Hmmm, this is not a creature I have seen. How pleasing he looks, but he's not like my Father at all. Have my thoughts wandered too far? Should I listen for Father?

Were you talking to me, creature? What did you say? That Father did not tell us all of the truth? . . . that we should know more, have more?

Restlessness.
 Jealousy.
  Discontentment.
   The fall.

Shadows block the rays streaming into the garden. Regret wells up a deep ache in us. The stillness is deafening. We stand naked, ashamed, and afraid. Father knows. Will we ever find our way back?

But God . . .

Eve had it all! I imagine she was beautiful. She was not tempted by restaurants on every corner or the Food Network. Because she ate the fruit and vegetables of the garden I am sure she had the creamiest of complexions. The apple of her husband's eye and living in the most beautiful place in the world, she knew

Father God face to face. She didn't have to work toward intimacy with her Father. She had it! Yet, she and her husband listened to Satan's spin about what God had or had not given her—that next thing out there. When Eve let her thoughts go, it brought discontentment to her heart as she began to question God's character of love. Did He have her best interest in mind? Was God holding out on her?

Why is it so hard to obey, trust, and rest in contentment? Because Paradise was lost.

But God . . .

"But the Lord called to the man" (Genesis 3:9) and God covered them. Father God was there to cover them. Their rebellion brought the fall and the first blood was shed to cover Adam and Eve. Rebellion was answered with sacrifice. They wandered away from Father's protective care and caused the very fall of mankind. Yet Father pointed the first family to His solution, to the blood of His Son, Jesus, who would pay for the sins of the world and send the Holy Spirit to dwell in us.

A Matter of the Heart

From this conversation in Eve's mind, the deception that led to discontentment began. Eve had the perfect parent and a great husband. She lived in paradise. Yet she desired the one thing she did not have and became discontented and jealous. Discontentment is not primarily a circumstantial problem.

It's a heart problem.

The Bible says the heart is exceedingly deceitful (Jeremiah 17:9). My heart, my thoughts, my feelings can lie to me. Left to *me* my heart lies. Regarding thoughts of the heart—studies show that men have about 20,000 and women have 40,000 thoughts pop through their minds each day.

Men and women think differently, as well. Men have the wonderful ability to compartmentalize and manage their thoughts. They can even think about nothing. What a gift. But unless a woman is sick or asleep, she is always thinking about something! It's easy to see why the devil approached Eve first.

God knows this is a tough assignment so His instruction is clear. The only way to win the battle is to take those thousands of thoughts captive to the obedience of Christ. To take captive is to imprison, lock up, or cage each of those lying thoughts, one at a time. God is telling us that our old way of thinking must be changed. These lying thoughts have to shut up! A lifetime of thinking patterns and perceptions can only be shut up by the Spirit of God and through His beautiful word. Through the Holy Spirit, God's words renew our mind and make us look more like Him one day and one season at a time.

Whose Voice?

There are two voices in the mind of a child of God—the voice of the Holy Spirit and the voice of self and Satan. An old Chinese proverb explains it well. "There is a good dog and a bad dog fighting within each of us. **The one that is going to win is the one we feed the most."**

The bad dog, a stranger, is the voice of desperation, confusion, worry, discontentment, fear, anger, frenzied panic, and an absolute determination to control. That's the voice we want to shut up. The good dog is the voice of the Holy Spirit, the Shepherd. His is the voice of peace, comfort, discernment, courage, warning, and direction.

Jesus described for us a shepherd and his sheep. "The sheep hear his voice and he calls his own sheep by name and leads them out. When he puts forth all his own, he goes ahead of them and the sheep follow him, because they know his voice. A stranger they simply will not follow but will flee from him, because they do not know the voice of strangers" (John 10:1-21).

This is absolutely true. I watched a video of people calling out to sheep. One at a time each person stepped up to the fence and called the sheep using the same words, voice inflection, and volume. One called, then another, and another.

The sheep did not move. They kept nibbling grass.

There was not a twitch until their own shepherd stepped up to the fence and called out to them using the same words, voice inflection, and volume. First one little sheep head popped up. Then another popped up to look. Then the entire flock ran to the voice of the shepherd.

I want to do that. I don't want to twitch toward any other voice.

I want to listen for His voice, and bound after Him when He calls.

Which dog, which voice is consuming my thoughts? The voice of discontentment, desperation, anger, fear, confusion, worry, need to control, and frenzied panic, or the voice of peace, hope, discernment, courage, joy, and purpose? Eve fell because she listened to the wrong voice. Yes, in order to hear something, we have to listen. Once Eve listened and pondered Satan's lies that God had not given her all she deserved, she and Adam with her followed the voice of the stranger.

If the children of the perfect parent fell from temptation to sin by listening to the stranger, so will we. So we cry out to The Helper, and by His Spirit we reel in a deceitful heart by taking our thoughts captive to the obedience of Christ. The following exemplifies one of those battles of the mind where the Shepherd had to draw me back to Him.

"He whose mind is stayed on Thee has perfect peace" . . .
He whose mind is not stayed on Thee does not.

It's three in the morning and I am thinking about friends and family and their needs. I think of a grief stricken young widow enduring her second sleepless night since she lost her husband. *Help her, Lord.* My thoughts move to our country. As a nation we moved away from God a long time ago and here we are. I grieve for the gifts God gave us that have been lost. I wonder if I am doing all I should for such a time as this.

Dana to God: Lord, Joseph listened for your voice and stored up grain for the seven years of famine, and even though he was mistreated and abused he delivered nations and ultimately his own family from destruction. What should we do, Lord? How much do we prepare for the famine that predictably occurs in every life or in a country? You know me, Lord. I can't keep too many balls in the air at one time. What do you want me to do?

God to Dana: He whose mind is stayed on Me has perfect peace.

Dana to God: "Lord this is so *not* perfect peace! Oh, Father. I come to you in the name of Jesus crying out that you help all of us, wrap your love around us, and give us courage and grace for each moment."

God to Dana: "Today, Dana. Trust me with today. "

Dana to God: "Yes. Thank you, for reminding me about today, Lord. Today is all my simple mind can deal with. You and Don are going to have to worry about tomorrow. Lord. You've got this, don't You?

God to Dana: Yes, Dana, I do.

Dana to God: One day at a time. In the season where I am living. Loving the person in front of me.

> For such a time as this.
> In Jesus name and by His Spirit.
> I love you, Lord. Good night."

It's a fight to rest contented in Christ, but get in the fight and stay there! God uses flawed people and He fulfills His promises to flawed people who struggle to believe Him. He did not love Eve, Peter, or John because of their perfect character. He loved and used them because of His perfect character. He loves us that way too.

Learning the Secret

We want to stay in this battle reeling in negative thoughts by filling our thoughts with God's and allowing His words to renew our mind. Then no matter what our circumstances are, our default will be—Jesus loves me. He's got this. Let's answer some questions about the thoughts making themselves at home in our minds.

1. Have you ever been driving down the street minding your own business and your thoughts turn to a person, a circumstance, or an offense? And these thoughts just won't go away. Perhaps someone is upset with us and we don't know how to fix it. Perhaps we get in a bad mood if we can't get your way. Do you quickly take offense or pass judgment? Do you have to blame someone for things that do not go the way you want them to? Is today never enough? Yikes! Though we may be so familiar with these emotions that they seem normal, they indicate a heart of discontentment. What might this look like for you?

_____

_____

2. Jesus told us we are to love Him not only with our hearts but also with our minds. This might be a good time to ask myself what is too often consuming my thoughts. Like the believers in

Corinth, what might be leading me away, tempting me again and again from my sincere and pure devotion to God? This, dear ones, is where the rubber meets the road. Let God show you where you are most snared in your thought life. What is He revealing to you?

_____

_____

3. Perhaps my temptations are showing me a place I have taken my eyes off my Shepherd and have stopped listening for Him. It's scary, but I might not even hear that still small voice leading me God's way in this area. Perhaps my all consuming thoughts are an idol of which I am totally unaware. It could be my phone, social networking, or TV. It could be the stock market, making money, food, worry, sports, shopping, kids, video games, news that takes me into a dark place, need to control, even the Food Network and exercise. Yes, even the good stuff can become a snare. Can you relate to any of these or recall an idol that is too great a part of your thoughts?

_____

_____

4. If so, the first step is to repent and then invite Christ to reside in that place. To repent is to change direction. Ask God to help you hear the Shepherd's voice. Ask Him to give you

discernment to recognize when you are listening to destructive or futile thoughts. And remember that confusion is never from God. Consciously decide what you will and will not listen to among the many thoughts passing through your mind. Consider that the good can be the enemy of the best. What are some steps you might need to take to take to begin to take your thoughts captive to the obedience of Christ?

_____

_____

5. Eve did not listen for the still small voice of her Father to draw her back to the protective covering of her husband or her God. Once she chose to engage in conversation with the enemy she was hooked. She began to then dwell on that thought, and it did not take much dwelling before she believed the lie and acted on it. Are there some lies you have believed perhaps most of your life that have caused sin patterns to take hold? What might they be?

_____

_____

6. Read Acts 2:14-36 for the full story of the coming of the Helper, the Paraclete that Jesus promised would come. Describe this event.

_____

_____

7. A pretty dramatic demonstration of God's power IN US, don't you think? The Holy Spirit could have gently and quietly rested on the followers of Christ, yet the event was unmistakably supernatural. Though many do not live like it, the Holy Spirit of the Living God resides in every true believer in Jesus Christ. Like Joshua though, we have to go in and fight for it. Read Joshua 1: 1-9. What does God tell Joshua to do in verse 8?

_____

_____

8. What does God tell Joshua three times in these verses?

_____

_____

We are not going to let the book of the law depart from our lips and we are going to be strong and courageous in Jesus' name!

9. Galatians 2:20 reminds us who we are, so we are going to plant this verse a little deeper in our hearts.

"I have been crucified with Christ and I no longer live, but Christ lives in me. The life I now live in the body, I live by faith in the Son of God, who loved me and gave Himself for me" Galatians 2:20).

I	L	T	T
H	I	L	S
B	M.	I	O
C		N	G,
W		L	W
C		I	L
A		T	M
I		B,	A
N		I	G
L		L	H
L		B	F
B		F	M
C		I	

Galatians 2:20

"Therefore I urge you brothers in view of God's mercy to offer your bodies as living sacrifices holy and pleasing to God—this is your spiritual act of worship. Do not conform any longer to the patterns of this world but be transformed by the renewing of your mind. Then you will be able to test and approve what God's will is, God's good pleasing and perfect will. Romans 12:1,2

T	S	A	M.	G
I	H	L	T	G
U	A	T	Y	P
Y	P	T	W	A
B	T	P	B	P
I	G-	O	A	W.
V	T	T	T	
O	I	W	T	
G	Y	B	A	
M	S	B	A	
T	A	T	W	
O	O	B	G	
Y	W.	T	W	
B	D	R	I,	
A	N	O		
L	C	Y		

Romans 12:1-2

Part 2
The Battle for Contentment

Introduction

The circumstances in which we live are the tip of the iceberg. The real war (Ephesians 6:10-20) is the 90% beneath the water that we can't see. The enemy of God wants the circumstances of life to keep us scurrying and worrying up in that 10% we see. His intent is to divert us through distraction and discouragement from a purposeful, intimate relationship with Jesus Christ. A semblance of relationship hindering us from making a difference in our world suits him very well. I believe though, that most of us desire to know God intimately—to truly know Him.

When I was a child we sang patriotic songs in school, and I loved them. I have sweet memories of being on my backyard swing, singing and swinging as high as I could for as long as I liked. My hair swooshed forward and back as I pumped my legs. The sky was big, and I was free. Leaning back, looking up at the beautiful sky I would sing at the top of my lungs, "O beautiful for spacious skies, for amber waves of grain, for purple mountains majesty above the fruited plain. America! America! God shed his grace on thee, and crown thy good with brotherhood from sea to shining sea." Spacious skies, amber waves, purple mountains, from one shining sea to another. They sounded beautiful.

I loved being under that spacious sky. Growing up in Texas, I know the big sky. I didn't know what amber waves, purple mountains, or those seas were though. My family had never driven outside Texas except on a few day trips across the border to Mexico. After my first year teaching fourth grade though, my husband and I piled into our baby blue VW bug along with our eighty-pound dog, Rusty, and headed to Colorado.

That evening while driving through Kansas we saw wheat fields ripe for harvest. The wind was blowing and as far as the eye could see were miles and miles of amber, yes, amber waves of grain! I had sung about amber waves. Now I knew what they were. When we came into eastern Colorado I looked for the mountains. I didn't know the fruited plain was in the east of the state and the mountains to the west. Later in the day as we traveled, the sun setting in the western sky, I saw for the first time purple mountains. They were majestic. Later while visiting our son, I saw those shining seas, one on the east coast, one on the west. I had sung about them. Now I knew what they were.

I in no way understood God's amazing grace, nor the richness of true brotherhood. As the days and season pass though, as deep, sweet waves of grace pour over my life, I have experienced them. It is one thing to know *about* something or someone. It is quite another to truly know it or them. Through the ages many religious folks have known God's word, yet they did not know Him. In our world today, many spout the words in The Book but do not know the Author of The Book. The word apart from God though, is powerless.

Satan knows that. So he doesn't mind religion at all. He is right in the middle of religion. He keeps religious folks busy with do's and do not's and doing, doing, doing banking on them missing God in the process. Jesus told the Pharisees, "You study the Scriptures diligently because you believe that in them you have eternal life. These are the very Scriptures that testify about Me, yet you refuse to come to Me to have life (John 5:39,40).

Like amber waves of grain, purple mountains, shining seas and God's grace, we don't want to know *about* our Father. We want to truly know Him. To know Him though, and to learn to hear

His voice and follow it, we are going to be in for a fight. Wars in history have a beginning and end, but this spiritual war in which we find ourselves is with us until the day we take our last breath and step over to the other side. Sadly, though we and those we love are the spoils of this war, many are ill-equipped for the battle or not even be aware it is going on.

In *the Lion, the Witch, and the Wardrobe* series, C.S. Lewis' wardrobe transports his characters into a parallel world without the time constraints in which we live. This world that they climb through the wardrobe to enter is a brilliant illustration of our invisible spiritual war.

Our hearts and minds don't operate in a spiritual vacuum. We are engaged in war whether we are aware of it or not. We can't just know *about* Jesus Christ. We need to climb through that wardrobe into Narnia. We need to dive beneath the water to the 90% of the iceberg we can't see. We need to engage in the real fight—the fight to intimately know our Jesus. It is a fight for intimacy that brings such contentment to us that we impact our world.

5

A Real Enemy

"The thief comes to kill, steal, and destroy"
John 10:10

A few years ago when I started writing these pages on the spiritual war, I pressed to get through them for many months. As I wrote those I loved most were neck deep in warfare, one literally at war, and some in the fights of their lives. Yes, we are in a war, and the stakes are as high as was the price for our victory—the very blood of Jesus Christ.

We know God will fulfill His promises to us because of what Jesus did on the cross. We know that if we are His children we have the very Spirit of the living God in us. Why then do we fail at trusting Him? Why is it hard to believe that what God says is true? Why do we become frightened, discouraged, and discontent?

Because we are in a war.

We have an enemy who wants to deceive, distract, disqualify, discourage, and cause division and fear. Our enemy, the devil, has one aim—to isolate and destroy us. On this side of eternity, the most blatant evidence of a diabolic power at work is the atrocities upon the innocent which seem to be growing increasingly wicked with each passing year. If we could see behind the spiritual curtain for a moment, it would perhaps shock us into action and engage us in this fight more real than what we see or feel.

We don't have to see behind the "spiritual" curtain to see horrible evil destroying the innocent of our world, though. Just turn on the nightly news, or check out some church prayer requests. Ultimately, we are fighting for a relationship of love with God and family. We're fighting for the kind of life of contentment and purpose that points a hurting world to Christ. It is all the same war and the same enemy. And there is a predictable path both to defeat and to victory.

The Devil

We don't want to give this enemy too much air time, but we do need to identify him. Who is this devil who has caused God's creation such harm through time? Matthew calls him the tempter (Matthew 4:3) and wicked one (Matthew 13:19). Luke refers to him as the enemy (Luke 10:19) and John, the prince of this world (John 12:31). Peter says he is your adversary the devil (1 Peter 5:8), and Paul, the prince of the power of the air (Ephesians 2:2). In the Revelation John's name for him is Apollyon or destroyer (Revelation 12:10).

The dictionary meaning for devil is accuser, slanderer, and deceiver. The name Satan appropriately means enemy of God. His many names describe his aim to destroy God's creation. He is alive and well, and he and his minions are operating on planet earth. Yet, his most effective deception is convincing the world he does not exist. He is therefore, above all else the father of lies, and though brilliant, not a creator, but an imitator.

Lucifer was the devil's name before the fall. He is called a morning star in Isaiah. "How you have fallen from heaven, o morning star, son of the dawn. You have been cast down to the earth, you who once laid low the nations" (Isaiah 14:12). In this passage, the King James Version of the Bible translates *morning star* as "Lucifer, son of the morning." It is clear from the rest of the passage that Isaiah is referring to the deceiver's fall from heaven. Satan was a created being, perhaps the most beautiful creation of God, probably the most powerful of all the angels.

The morning star is Venus. I remember wondering why God gave the devil that beautiful name, one I felt he did not deserve even before his fall. After all, Venus is the brightest and most beautiful star in the sky in the early morning. I later learned that the devil was "a" morning star. Jesus Christ is referred to as "The" Morning Star.

Perhaps God called the angel who would rebel "a" morning star, because though Venus is bright and beautiful just before dawn and is brilliant in the morning sky, as the sun rises, Venus diminishes quickly until it totally disappears. Though the devil appears brilliant and effective in his destruction as he roams the earth, in the light of *The Son*, he diminishes and completely disappears. He is a cheap imitation of "The" Morning Star. Keep that in mind as we learn a few things about the devil and his strategy.

Jesus is "The" Bright Morning Star and outshines all other stars. And in regard to our life and walk with God, as the Son of God grows in us, Satan's influence and power diminishes. "In regard to judgment the prince of this world, Lucifer stands condemned" (John 16:11).

His days are numbered.

Amen to that, Lord.

The devil's days are numbered. But he is evil *and* present. When I was a young woman I heard the testimony of a Christian woman who had been a witch before she was saved. Yes, witches are real. This woman was reared by Satanists, and her testimony gave me a perspective of the spiritual war I can never forget. I won't go into the evil against the innocent that she shared with us. But she thoroughly described the devil's evil doings, citing specifically the occult's two high holy days, the spring and fall solstice. The fall solstice is Halloween. I was raising my boys alone and was not a risk-taker at my boldest. I didn't want anything to do with a night sold out to the devil. So for the boys and me Halloween was a movie and popcorn night.

Looking back, I wish I had not hunkered in the bunker. We are God's children and every day *and* night belongs to Him. If the hurting of the world are out on Halloween, I think we Christians armed in the armor of God should be, as well. Jesus is the light of the world. He lives in us, so *we* go into dark places to be light.

Our church encourages us to have cookouts in our driveways on this night as an outreach to our neighbors. My children and their families touch the lives of folks in their neighborhoods on Halloween. Most Halloweens nowadays, I'm in a driveway with my kids and grandkids with a yes face reaching out with hotdogs, a smile, and a God bless you.

Above all on Halloween and every day, I need to be prayerful and purposeful. This is the time to pray! If the occult is pulling out all the big guns this time of the year, so should we. We should be praying for our families *and* our neighbors, so that when we open our door with a smile and a God bless you, God will have gone out to the battle before us wooing hearts to Him.

The Fall Before the Fall

Lucifer rebelled and fell before he tempted Adam and Eve to rebel and fall. This first rebellion was about a prideful creation. In Isaiah 14, Lucifer says repeatedly, "I will . . . I will . . . I will . . . ." In his proclamations of what he would do Lucifer displayed pride—the pride which makes us think we are smarter, more beautiful, more wounded, more worthy, more unworthy, or more whatever than we really are. This was a dead end for him. It's a dead end for us.

This most beautiful of the angels got the big head. He wanted to be God, and pride always comes before a fall. As with decisions we make, others' eyes were watching this leader angel. And the moment rebellion was conceived in Lucifer, a third of the angelic hosts followed him. I picture these radiantly beautiful heavenly beings turning into putrid, impish creatures (think Smeagol in the *Lord of the Rings*). Because evil cannot dwell in the presence of our holy God, the demons were immediately cast from Heaven. Satan, therefore, had his eye on God's children to destroy them from the moment they were created.

From the first temptation, the strategy of the enemy was to twist the truth just enough to pervert it, to spin it. Satan, the king of spin, took the truth of God's word and twisted it ever so little, making it a lie. He knows that just a twist makes the truth a lie. So must we.

Look back at that scene in the garden from Genesis 3. "The serpent was craftier than any of the wild animals the Lord God had made. He said to the woman, 'Did God *really* say you must not eat from any tree in the garden?' The woman said to the serpent, 'We may eat fruit from the trees in the garden, but God did say, you must not eat fruit from the tree that is in the middle of the garden, and you must not touch it, or you will die.' 'You will surely not die,' the serpent said to the woman. 'For God knows that when you eat of it, your eyes will be opened, and you will be like God, knowing good and evil" (Genesis 3:1-5).

There it is. "Did God *really* say?"

Just a twist of God's words plants a seed of doubt in Eve's mind.

Wandering Off

Eve showed disrespect for her husband and for her God. Why did her mind wander off and why in the world didn't Adam step up and tell her, 'no'? Both were out from under God's protective authority and it left their hearts vulnerable to attack. Though resting under my husband's spiritual covering sometimes cramps my style, and at times I balk, it is the safest and sweetest place for me to reside. And though it is difficult for a man to lead a woman who doesn't want to submit to him, his wife and family are safest when he is the spiritual leader of his family.

Perhaps Eve felt alone, and isolation renders us victims. Lambs, babies, Christians out of fellowship with God and others . . . all are vulnerable. When we isolate ourselves from the body of Christ, we become easy prey for the roaring lion.

Don't let disillusionment and discontent with people drive you away from the church. Christians are a bunch of sinners who will sorely disappoint us along the way. But we are family. We are Christ's body. And just as a finger or toe will die if disconnected from the body, so will we. We don't need isolation but the insulation the body of Christ provides. We need people to pray with, to pray for, and to do life with. We need each other.

Eye on the Shepherd

We don't have to become fixated on our enemy to keep from wandering off though. We just need to know enough about him to understand his attack and intent. Our pastor shares an analogy regarding counterfeit bills that puts this into perspective. The way a banker learns to recognize a counterfeit bill is not by studying counterfeits, but by studying the real thing. Then when a counterfeit bill passes through a bank employee's hands, he immediately recognizes it for what it is.

We stay close to the Shepherd and keep our eyes on Him because the best way to recognize deception, temptation, and stupid thinking for what it is, is to have our eyes on the real thing, on Jesus. We read the word of God and listen for His voice *so much* that when the liar speaks, we immediately recognize who he is. Satan must bow to the word of God. So his greatest threats are Christians who know and believe their Bibles and talk to their Father in Heaven—about everything!

To defeat an enemy we have to first identify him and then we need to engage him. But we must engage the devil God's way, fighting with God's spiritual arsenal in place and through the power of the Holy Spirit.

By His Spirit.

It's easy to lose sight of this. I spend a lot of time looking in the mirror trying to smooth things down and lift things up to feel relatively attractive before heading out the door. Sometimes I succeed. Sometimes I do not. What I spend so much time looking at though, is just the wrapping paper. The gift is on the inside! We are not a body with a spirit in it. We are a spirit being with a body wrapped around it. The wrapping paper is fading away but the gift is growing day by day into the likeness of Christ.

Because we are spirit, we fight in the Spirit! Or do we?

The Fight's Below the Water

Do we fight in the Spirit? How much do we really dive into the water and get into the spiritual fight waged against us? The Lord said the battle is His. Am I allowing the God of the universe to fight my battles or am I fighting them in my own strength and understanding? The infamous story of the sinking of the Titanic is a reminder of the effects of ignoring the real threat below the water.

In April of 1912, this most elegant of luxury ships was on its maiden voyage. It was the largest ship afloat at the time and was filled with some of the wealthiest people in the world, as well as many emigrants from Europe heading to a new life in America. The surroundings were splendid for the first class guests. The suites, dining rooms, and ballrooms were opulent. No expense had been spared as the finest service in the world was offered. Each of the passengers on the Titanic, whether rich or poor, was excitedly confident of smooth sailing and a bright tomorrow.

This magnificent vessel, though beautiful, teeming with life, and moving swiftly across the ocean, was heading into dangerous waters filled with icebergs. Just ten percent of them were above water and visible. Ninety percent of the danger lurked below; a danger that was real whether they were aware of it or not. Because the crew did not concern themselves with that notable ninety percent, it took the ship under.

Paul wrote specifics to the Corinthian church about how to pray, to believe God, and to fight. "For though we live in the world, we do not wage war as the world does. The weapons we fight with are not the weapons of the world. On the contrary they have divine power to demolish strongholds. We demolish arguments and every pretension that sets itself up against the knowledge of God, and we take captive every thought to make it obedient to Christ" (2 Corinthians 10: 3-5).

We can't fight with weapons of this world. Only the weapon *not* of this world, which is God's word, has the power to demolish strongholds and take our thoughts captive to the obedience of Christ. God's word and relationship with Him change our thinking, and the more we get to know Him, the more we trust and believe that His ways work. The battle at Satan's rebellion, in the Garden of Eden, throughout the Old Testament, with our Lord Jesus in the desert, at Gethsemane, at the cross, and to the resurrection is the same battle we fight today. This bears repeating. Neither Satan's strategy nor God's mysterious and wonderful solution have changed.

The adversary's intent in every temptation since the first is to get us to question the character of God and to grow jealous and discontent. When we question God's character, Satan is waiting to move into our thoughts. He fools us by exchanging the truth with a lie, so he can break our fellowship with the Lord for a while. This is when we get into trouble.

We get to know someone by spending time with them. The sad fact is that most professing Christians do not spend much time with their God. If that sticks in our craw, it should. Studies have shown that on average, pastors spend about four to five minutes per day reading their Bibles, and these minutes are usually only for sermon preparation. Four to five minutes per day in their Bibles? God help us! No wonder we are in such a mess, with blind shepherds leading blind sheep. Perhaps we are far too familiar with the voice of the bad dog.

The deceiver wants to keep me busy, out of the Book, and off our knees. To know Him though, I need to stay close Him. I need to allow Him to renew my mind so I won't be listening to the bad dog's lies any longer.

Then when worrying or negative thoughts come, I will more likely turn them to prayer. I will sift my thoughts and circumstances through what God says, and then pray for the person, the circumstance, or the worry. If the Shepherd has allowed my thoughts to go that way, He's the reason I thought about it in the first place!

A thought, then a prayer!

I was reminded of the spiritual war waging when I stepped in the door of our son's home one afternoon. I heard his kids singing a chorus I had often heard them sing before as they marched through the house. *"Shut the door, Keep out the devil. Shut the door. Keep the devil in the night."*

It reminded me of a day when our sons were in high school and we first heard this chorus. That morning a group of young men from Africa performed in chapel. We watched them dressed in their beautiful native shirts, rhythmically as only they could, harmonize and dance their way through the gym. This chorus was unforgettable for all of us, and Chris had taught it to his children.

The words were simple, poignant, and powerful. They were a warning, an admonition and an encouragement for a gym full of American high school kids and for us. Because these African children had grown up around the occult and evil practices in their everyday life, they knew who their enemy was. They knew to engage him. They knew to shut the door and keep the devil in the night. They knew that on this side of that door is God's light and intimacy with The Shepherd.

Learning the Secret

1. Write out these scriptures that reveal the enemy's work against us:

   Matthew 4:3:

   _____

   _____

   Matthew 13:19:

   _____

   _____

   John 12:31:

   _____

   _____

   1 Peter 5:8:

   _____

   _____

Ephesians 2:2:

_____

_____

2. In Isaiah 14:13-14 what did Lucifer say he would do?

_____

_____

In Isaiah 14:12, 15, what did God do in response to his rebellion?

_____

_____

_____

3. Write out Proverbs 16:18:

_____

_____

Yup! Don't mess with God!

4. How does a follower of the Shepherd, Jesus, wage this war against the enemy of God? 2 Corinthians 10:3-5

_____

_____

   a. What kind of power do these weapons have?

_____

_____

   b. What do they demolish?

_____

_____

   c. What do they take captive?

_____

_____

Here are more of God's powerful words to hide in your heart.

"For though we live in the world, we do not wage war as the world does. The weapons we fight with are not the weapons of the world. On the contrary they have divine power to demolish strongholds. We demolish arguments and every pretension that sets itself up against the knowledge of God, and we take captive every thought to make it obedient to Christ"
2 Corinthians 10: 3-5

F	N	W	W.	D	S	W
T	W	F	O	S.	I	T
W	W	W	T	W	U	C
L	A	A	C	D	A	E
I	T	N	T	A	T	T
T	W	T	H	A	K	T
W,	D.	W	D	E	O	M
W	T	O	P	P	G	T
D	W	T	T	T	A	C

2 Cor. 10:3-5

6

Our Defense—The Armor of God

"Finally, be strong in the Lord and in His mighty power. Put on the full armor of God, so that you can take your stand against the devil's schemes. For our struggle is not against flesh and blood, but against the rulers, against the authorities, against the powers of this dark world and against the spiritual forces of evil in the heavenly realms. Therefore put on the full armor of God, so that when the day of evil comes, you may be able to stand your ground, and after you have done everything, to stand. Stand firm then, with the belt of truth buckled around your waist, with the breastplate of righteousness in place, and with your feet fitted with the readiness that comes from the gospel of peace. In addition to all this, take up the shield of faith, with which you can extinguish all the flaming arrows of the evil one. Take the helmet of salvation and the sword of the Spirit, which is the word of God"

Ephesians 6:10-1.

In this passage Paul is calling us to action and instructs us twice to put on the full armor of God. There are no exclamation marks in these ancient texts; the repetition of a concept is for absolute emphasis. Paul tells them, "You think you are fighting people and circumstances, but you are fighting the enemy of God, so *put on your armor*!

Three times Paul instructs us to STAND urging us never to give up! If I am a child of God—truth, righteousness, peace, faith, and the joy of my salvation should be growing in me, "so that when the day of evil comes you may be able to stand your ground." Don't miss that.

Paul prepares us with the appropriate word, not *if*, but *when* the evil day comes. No matter who we are, what we know or don't know, how much money or education we have or do not have, where we go to church, or who we work for, *evil days will come*. Without God's defense in place, we are at the mercy of our enemy. Therefore, we should to be prepared to stand.

God made us, and He wrote our instruction manual, the Bible, with rules under which our lives will bear fruit. Among these rules is provision for both a defense and an offense for this invisible war. These rules for battle help us understand and fight for relationship with God and family, and for a purposeful life that points a hurting world to Jesus Christ—this life of contentment.

Why does God exemplify attributes for our defense with pieces of armor? Why armor? Armor exhibits protection and preparedness. We need to be prepared for anything: for study, for playing a sport, for marriage, for a job, a project, a performance, to prepare a great meal, *and* for war. Either literal armor or a type of armor must be in place for us to succeed.

The nation of Israel is surrounded by enemies on every side growing more hostile with each passing year. But Israel's government has something in place called the Iron Dome. The Iron Dome is their armor. It is a defense system that intercepts missiles in midair which have been launched from other countries in the Middle East. The Iron Dome protects lives in Israel every single day.

For decades a strong standing Army, Navy, Air force, Marine Corp, and Coast Guard have kept the United States of America safe whether we had troops deployed or not. We have some chinks in our armor right now, a weakened military which needs to be shored up. Because the world that is, is not the world that was, and is not the world that will be, we need a strong military defense. A nation with a strong defense makes an enemy far less willing to cross its borders and invade. So is our need for a strong defense against Satan, the enemy of our souls and the enemy of the Christian family.

I learned about a type of armor, berry-pickin' armor, when my mother took my brother Tim and I to pick dewberries. I didn't know that those dewberry picking trips were teaching us to be prepared, but they were. Houston summers are hot and humid. There is not a hint of breeze unless a quick shower blows through. So from the time school ended in May I was barefoot and wearing shorts and a t-shirt.

I didn't understand Momma's insistence that we put on jeans, long sleeved shirts, socks, shoes, and even gloves. It seemed ridiculous to me. I hadn't thought about protecting myself from the elements. I just wanted to fill my bucket to the brim with berries and get back home for a shower, some air-conditioning, and a bowl of berries and cream. Momma grew up on a farm though. As a little girl she had learned how to work *and* how to be prepared for work. She knew how to dress to harvest in a place filled with mosquitoes, chiggers, thorns, and poison ivy.

On that first trip, I learned there was more to berry picking than just picking berries. First we had to get to the berry patch. We drove a good distance and then walked a long way across ditches and through weeds and pokey things. We were sweating bullets before we even got to the patch.

We finally began picking. We picked and picked until we got the berries within easy reach. Then we took off our gloves and reached deep into the bushes for big ripe berries. Our bare hands got scratched and bloody from the thorns. Our neck, arms, and legs were protected though. Our wise mother knew something about being prepared for battle against the enemies of berry pickers. Our clothes, though uncomfortable, protected us. We children of God need spiritual clothes, as well. That is the purpose for the armor. Without our spiritual armor in place, we and our families are sure to get scratched, chewed up, and poisoned.

Belt or Girdle of Truth

"Stand firm then, with the belt of truth buckled around your waist . . ."
Ephesians 6:14

Truth.

We begin with truth.

Truth, sincerity, authenticity: these are our girdle, our belt that holds our life together. Matthew Henry calls truth "sincerity in the inward parts." It holds all the other pieces of the armor and is therefore mentioned first in the scripture. Think about the purpose of a belt. A belt holds our britches up or a tunic together so it won't flap in the breeze. As a Christian I should be joyful because I am God's child, and that joy should be evident to my world. But the next most powerful witness to those I touch each day is that I am a person of truth – a person who speaks truth and knows The Truth.

Some might say, "It doesn't matter whether I know what is in the Bible or not. I am a Christian and I know a whole lot of stuff about God. I don't seem to get anything out of it anyway." Really? Every week that we take in more of the world than the word of God, we become more like the world. I have the mannerisms of and the more than copious nose of my family of origin. I am going to look like a Burke and emulate my world just by getting out of bed in the morning. It is only as I stay in the Word of God in communion with my Father in Heaven that I look more like Jesus. So I need to fill myself with the truth and seek to be a person of impeccable truth. My pastor teaches that this ethical truth is evidence of a transformed life. Believers should not have a separate personal life and public life. It should be the same life.

This quote has hung on my refrigerator for years. *"Life makes up its mind at home…whoever I am at home, is who I am!"* What if I am a total grouch with my husband—forgetting to take a breath and speak gently to him? What if I insist on putting my agenda above any of his needs? What if because I haven't had my shower yet, I disgustedly answer the door when a neighbor comes knocking instead of smoothing back my dirty hair and cheerfully inviting them in?

All I have to do is head over to that refrigerator and, bam— I get a little dose of reality. Whoever I am at home truly is who I am. If my children and grandchildren and those whom my life touches each day are going to walk in the truth, I must first, with all my heart, seek to walk in the truth before them.

Truth begins with understanding that God is God and we are not. Truth holds a life and a family together. Deception breaks us apart. If we want to become lovers of Christ and seek to raise authentic lovers of Jesus, we must first start with knowing and seeking to live His truth, secondly thinking and speaking the truth, and finally looking at ourselves and others through eyes of truth. **Whether we choose to live like we believe it or not, all life operates under the design of our Creator's truth.**

Being a Person of Truth

The truth of the word is like a flashlight into my heart. When I read the word I can see whether or not I have the belt of truth in place. When I read, *"If you say you love me, but hate your brother, you are a liar and the truth is not in you,"* I have to ask myself, "Do I love people, or do I hate them? Am I willing to forgive, do I harbor jealousies, am I prejudiced?"

It doesn't matter a bit what my selfish heart or the culture dictates. The question is: what does God say? When these attitudes are present in me, the truth is not in me. That is why I must honestly and regularly check that piece of armor and ask myself, "Am I walking in truth?"

Speaking Truth

Regarding the importance of truth, think of how violated you feel when someone lies to you. Maybe it was a quick *yes* that you knew very well was *no*. Perhaps it was a story that grew and grew with the telling, or maybe it was a destructive, blatant lie. When I realize someone has not been truthful with me, it hurts my heart. I no longer trust them.

Be courageous enough to ask yourself, "Do I tell the truth?" Perhaps as a child you learned to lie to keep the peace or protect yourself or someone else. Maybe you heard your parents lying and it was just a way of life, or you lied to get what you wanted.

We live in a culture increasingly saturated with lies. Lying makes you nervous, always looking over your shoulder trying to get your story straight. It makes you sick of mind and body. The devil loves it. If you struggle with telling the truth, as He can with all of our sins, God can fix that. You simply acknowledge it as sin and repent.

The tempter is so after our children, a generation of kids who are totally immersed in situational ethics. There is no standard. Or I should say the standard moves whenever it is convenient? I have cried and prayed over this as I have watched many being deceived and becoming deceivers themselves as they are led into Satan's grasp. It does not have to be this way though. We are the commanding officers of our families. We are in charge.

Our children need the security and example of our leading them counter-culture through a life of truth. Everyone in our world needs to see us speaking the truth.

Truth about Myself and Others

Finally, regarding truth, I need to face the truth about myself and others.

This is when we are going to grow up. Too many of us are afraid to say we have problems and need help. But admitting that bit of truth is where authenticity begins. We all have our snares, but as we grow in our relationship with our Lord we should become more real . . . more real with ourselves about who we are and with others.

This is not an easy order because we are by our sinful nature masters of disguise *and* liars. Remember Adam and Eve hiding in the garden? Though all of us are drawn to real-deal people, many of us hide what is inside. Children are drawn to authenticity too, and when they see compromise in their role models it can destroy their faith in God and us. The surest way our precious kids will learn to walk in freedom is that they observe truth, even truth about our struggle with sin, with no compromise, no smorgasbord, no pickin' and choosin' in our lives.

When you walk through my front door one of the first things you will see is a wall hanging with 3 John 4 written on it. *"I have no greater joy than to hear that my children are walking in the truth."* It is my greatest desire and joy to know that my loved ones continue the struggle to walk God's way, in the truth.

Satan knows that truth sets us free, and he doesn't want us to walk in freedom. So, we who professes Jesus Christ as Lord must seek with all that is within us not to cancel the power of the gospel by the way we live before others. Our kids are vulnerable to things they have seen and experienced through the media, at school, and beyond. From family they need the comfort of truth in love to hold on to.

Let us daily make our aim, by the grace of God, to be a person resting in that secure place of truth.

Lord, May I and my family be people of truth. May we believe and walk in God's truth. May we speak the truth. May we believe the truth about ourselves and others. If we are deceived in any way, Lord, please show us the truth so we will walk with hearts pure and free before You.

Breastplate of Righteousness

"...with the breastplate of righteousness in place..." (v. 14)

The dictionary meaning for "righteousness" is *virtue, decency, honesty, uprightness, doing right, or the courage to do the right thing*. So why is righteousness a breastplate? A breastplate protects the heart. You can't miss it. It's right out front protecting not only the heart but all the vital organs. Proverbs 13:6 reads, "Righteousness guards a man of integrity." Wow! When I do the right thing it protects my heart and the hearts of those around me! Doing right today plants seeds of blessing for my tomorrows.

How can this be if apart from Christ I have no righteousness in me? How can God declare *me* the righteousness of Christ? Under the provision of God's justice, someone had to pay the penalty for my sin, and it was Jesus. His blood was the payment for my righteousness. Though there is no righteousness in me, God wrapped Christ's righteousness around me. Now when God sees me, He sees Jesus. Matthew Henry wrote that God has implanted [righteousness] in us which fortifies us against the attacks of the enemy.

Our salvation doesn't depend on our righteousness, but God's. I don't have to prove my righteousness, He already has. I just believe. "Abraham believed God and God counted him righteous because of his faith" (Romans 4 and Galatians 3). He counts us righteous by His work on the cross, and this breastplate guards our hearts, providing an environment in which our righteous life grows.

"The path of righteousness is like the first gleam of dawn, shining ever brighter till the full light of day"
Proverbs 4:18

Because we are the very righteousness of Christ, we have the power within us to do the right thing. When we feel unworthy or beaten down, remember that we are God's children purchased with the blood of Christ. So pick up the breastplate and put it on. It has been paid for in full.

How do I do that? I do it first by knowing what is right from God's word. If I don't read the instruction manual, the love letter from God, I won't know what is right. I plan ahead to do right, relying on the power of God to do it. When I fail, I ask for God's forgiveness and mercy, and for the power to do the right thing. God does not ask of us anything He will not give us the power to do. "God has given us all we need for life and godliness" (2 Peter 1:3).

Lord, I and those I love are the righteousness of Christ because of You. May the righteousness that we possess affect every area of our lives. May we be known as people who conduct ourselves in a right manner not because we have to, but because we want to do it for Christ sake, knowing that we have the very power of God in us to do so.

Greaves (Brass Shoes) -The Gospel of Peace

"...and with your feet fitted with the readiness that comes from the gospel of peace..." (v. 15)

This peace Christ left us is fitted to our feet from our Father—it's personal. We can't get that fitting over the phone or on line, or even from a good Bible teacher if that is all we are relying on. God fits us with His peace as we know Him and live in light of the cross of Christ. That is what makes us ready, ready for each day and what it may bring, ready for this season of life.

Any good warrior needs his feet taken care of. Any successful athlete needs the right kind of shoes. In any profession, the proper footwear is important, because our feet are our foundation. Shoes or greaves of brass were part of military armor in ancient times and protected against gall traps and sharp sticks. Soldiers who ran across these traps unprotected were rendered unfit to march.

The preparation of the gospel of peace "signifies a prepared and resolved frame of heart to adhere to the gospel and abide by it which will enable us to walk with a steady pace in our walk with Christ" (Matthew Henry Commentary). Resolving to walk in that peace which passes understanding gives us fuel for the race.

As Jesus explained the promise of the Holy Spirit to His disciples, He said, "Peace I leave with you, my peace I give you. I do not give you as the world gives. Do not let your hearts be troubled and do not be afraid" (John 14:27). He left His peace with us. It is part of our heritage, a fruit of His Holy Spirit.

Paul told us to be strong in the Lord and His mighty power. In order to walk in His mighty power I need to be close in relationship to my Shepherd, listening, trusting, and obeying. Knowing the battle is the Lord's, and my armor is in place, I can stand against the devil just like Jesus did in the desert, and when I have done everything . . .

I stand.

"A quiet and peaceable mind, not easily provoked, nor prone to quarrel, but gentle and long suffering to all men . . . . This will certainly preserve you from many great temptations and persecutions as did those shoes of brass the soldiers from those gall traps" (Matthew Henry Commentary).

We stand on the peace you left us at the cross. Lord, give us and ours that peace today, so that no matter what happens, it will hold us up. May there be sweetness in our homes, unity in our families, and love that is obvious as we and those who watch our lives experience the peace of Christ which passes all understanding. Father, please protect us and give us joy and a thankful heart in living each day. And, Lord, grow us up in the truth of your beautiful word. In Jesus' name I pray, Amen

Shield of Faith

"In addition to all this, take up the shield of faith, with which you can extinguish all the flaming arrows of the evil one" (v. 16) remembering that "faith is the substance of things hoped for evidence of things not seen" Hebrews 11:1

E. M. Bounds describes faith as, ". . . the foundation of Christian character and the security of the soul" (*Prayer and Spiritual Warfare* p.9). Our faith is the foundation of our character. Hebrews 11:6 reads, "And, without faith it is impossible to please God."

This life is called a faith walk.

We have been given a measure of faith by God, His gift to us. Our faith, our choosing to believe, is more necessary than any other part of the defensive armor. The breastplate secures our vital organs, but the shield turns toward the attack. Our faith is what gives us victory over the world. When these verses were written, both the Greek and the Roman soldiers had used shields. They formed what was called phalanx, with each man's shield hooked to the next. As long as the line did not break, it was almost impenetrable.

Our faith, believing what God says is true, shields us from the attack of the enemy. (One more time, Satan hates Christians who actually believe God, because our trust in what the Lord says deflects attacks intended for us and ours). When we pray with others, we are joining our shields with theirs, and it is powerful! *"Though one may be overpowered, two can defend themselves. A chord of three strands is not quickly broken."* (Ecclesiastes. 4:12)

We don't need to conjure up our faith or work ourselves up in a frenzy though, because our faith is not in our faith. The source of our faith is Jesus Christ. He has given us enough faith to take Him at His word. Our faith is our shield. Hold it up! As I was praying for a tough situation, I opened my Bible and the Lord showed me things I had not seen before. He showed me a different way to pray for this situation. It sounded good, and as always I began to share my heart with Him.

Dana to God: *But honesty, Lord, I am so weary. I read what you are showing me. I know it is from You to me, but . . .* Then I remembered what I had taught my class that morning. I had told them to hold up the shield of faith. That is what stops those fiery darts.

Dana to God: *What does it mean, Lord, to hold up the shield of faith?* Then I began to say out loud, "I do believe what your word says, Lord, not the fear of the circumstances that is trying to camp in my gut. I know this fight is not against flesh and blood but against spiritual forces in high places. I believe You."

As I spoke out those words, peace followed *and* then courage. Because my shield of faith was up, though I had no idea where it came from, I stood right up and prayed a courageous prayer. In Peter's second epistle, he describes the growth in the life of a follower of Christ who is becoming more like Jesus. Peter starts with faith. ". . . make every effort to add to your faith goodness, and to goodness, knowledge, and to knowledge, self-control, and to self control perseverance, and to perseverance godliness and to godliness brotherly kindness and to brotherly kindness, love" (2 Peter 1:5,6). From faith comes goodness, knowledge, self-control and all the rest. We start with faith by picking up our shield and *choosing* to live by faith not by feelings.

Lord, we know it starts with faith. Our faith shields us, so help me get that shield up. Help us to believe You, Lord, when there are voices all around that are contrary to Your truth. Give us the faith to believe and respond to your love. Lord. We know our faith absolutely protects our hearts from the attacks of the enemy, so we choose to believe You.

Helmet of Salvation

"Take the helmet of salvation" (v. 17) . . . It's a free gift.

A helmet protects our heads from death blows. Our salvation brought us from death to life and no one can take that life from us. But the devil will try to convince us otherwise. When he says, "You aren't good enough to be God's kid. You can't do that and belong to Jesus," throw those thoughts right back at him. If we are His, we are His!

It is important to remember though, that all the benefits of God such as the armor are reserved for the King's kids. Religion will not get us membership into this club. Relationship will. The fact that Jesus is our Savior should bring us joy, the joy of our salvation. Might we check out this piece of armor to make sure it is secure? Am I God's child? If I am, then it is settled.

Yet some folks may ask God the same questions they have for years. "Well, I prayed for this and I prayed for that, but nothing ever seems to work out. Why won't God give me a break!" Theirs is a life of disappointment in God. No matter what they do, or how hard they work, things just don't seem to work out. God let's them down again and again. They may pray. But they rarely read their Bibles for themselves, so they don't know what's in there. Maybe . . . they don't know Who is in there. With no joy and no idea how to see God's good, pleasing and perfect will, they are unaware they are living without God's armor in place. They are confused about their purpose and totally vulnerable when the evil day comes.

Life in Christ is joy—not always ease, but joy. If I am a child of God, do I allow myself to enjoy Him? Am I becoming a more joyful person through the years? This is not happiness based on circumstances, or the next thing I bring home from a shopping trip, or accomplish at work, but joy even when there is no job or no money for a shopping trip. Joy for no other reason than that I belong to Him.

Lord I pray for the salvation of each of my family members and children. I pray that if they have prayed to receive You, but it is not a true conversion, that You will, as the months and years go by, show them. Lord, draw my loved ones to You. Bring their thoughts from self to You, Lord, and give us all eternal perspective as we walk in the joy of our salvation. In Jesus' name.

Learning the Secret

Some of these questions may make you nervous, and you may be new at this, but remember—your answers are between you and God. And it is exciting to get honest with God because truth sets us free!

1. If someone asked me what I have read in God's word today, this week, this month, what would I tell them? What is God showing you through your answer?

_____

_____

2. What impact does my being/not being in the word of God have on my family and those significant others, as well as my response to life?

_____

_____

3. If I'm not making time to spend with God, what steps can I take to change that?

_____

_____

4. Do I know enough of God's truth to know if my family has on the armor of God or that I do?

_____

_____

5. Am I a person of truth?

_____

_____

_____

6. Do I have personal (private) and public integrity? Am I the same person at home, in the car, at church, etc?

_____yes_____

_____

7. If I have become the righteousness of Christ, am I seeking to think and live like I am?

_____yes_____

_____

8. Do I plan ahead of time to do right, even if I am the only one who does? Do I teach my children to do right even if they are the only ones who are? (Living for an audience of ONE.)

_____

_____

9. Are my "peace shoes" securely in place? In other words, do I pursue peace and seek to bring the peace of Christ into the circumstances of my life even if they are tough ones? Or am I divisive, defensive, a griper, or a trouble-maker?

_____

_____

10. Can I honestly say I want to live by faith? If so, what does that mean? What does that look like for me?

_____

_____

"Finally, be strong in the Lord and in His mighty power. Put on the full armor of God, so that you can take your stand against the devil's schemes. For our struggle is not against flesh and blood, but against the rulers, against the authorities, against the powers of this dark world and against the spiritual forces of evil in the heavenly realms. Therefore, put on the full armor of God, so that when the day of evil comes, you may be able to stand your ground, and after you have done everything, to stand. Stand firm then, with the belt of truth buckled around your waist, with the breastplate of righteousness in place, and with your feet fitted with the readiness that comes from the gospel of peace. In addition to all this, take up the shield of faith, with which you can extinguish all the flaming arrows of the evil one. Take the helmet of salvation and the sword of the Spirit, which is the word of God" (Ephesians 6:10-17).

Choose some of these verses you want to hide in your heart. Write your vertical letters and get started!

7

Our Offense—the Word

God has provided us with His sword for close combat. Our sword is our only offensive weapon and it is both sword and His love letter to us. His word instructs us to "Take the helmet of salvation and the sword of the Spirit, which is the word of God" (Ephesians 6: 17). We are to take it, and to take it we pick it up, read it, and in the power of His Spirit we live it.

Why is the Word of God compared to a sword? In the first century Roman soldiers used a lightweight sword, approximately eighteen inches long, called a gladius. It was their primary weapon and was designed for close combat. God's word is our close combat weapon. "For the word of God is living and active and sharper than any two-edged sword, and piercing as far as the division of soul and spirit, of both joints and marrow, and able to judge the thoughts and intentions of the heart. And there is no creature hidden from His sight, but all things are open and lay bare to the eyes of Him with whom we have to give account (Hebrews 4:12). Wow!

First, God's word is a mirror into my heart. Like the Roman gladius this sword is double edged and cuts through the bunk of my life. It cuts through bad teaching, sin, thought patterns, brokenness, and spiritual sludge with which the enemy weighs me down. In an earlier chapter, we talked about using His word to take every thought captive to the obedience of Christ. All scripture is inspired by God. Yes, inspired by the Spirit of the Living God. He overshadowed the collaboration of the canon in the early church when leaders put together the writings of the New Testament. God gave us His words, and God preserved the words He gave us.

The longer I read the Bible the more I see that it is reliable and true. The Bible agrees with itself. When I have a question about one scripture, another scripture I read later answers that question. There have been times when I have read the word and thought, *What in the world is God talking about?* or *I wonder why He did that?* only to later find a fresh nugget that answers my question. The Bible is the best commentary on the Bible. The pieces fit perfectly. "Every word of God is flawless. . . (Proverbs 30:5a). This text in Proverbs goes on to read, "He is a shield to those who take refuge in Him. Do not add to his words or He will rebuke you and prove you a liar" (Proverbs 30:5b, 6). So we stick close to our Shepherd, take refuge in Him and never mess with His book!

At the end of The Revelation God gives this warning, "If anyone adds anything to them, God will add to that person the plagues described in this scroll" (Revelation 22:18). We don't add to God's word. We are God's children and the apple of His eye. Adding any work or requirement to God's grace is a false message that leads us back into bondage.

"And if anyone takes words away from this scroll of the prophecy, God will take away from that person any share in the tree of life and in the Holy City" (Revelation 22:19). That's losing heaven, and that's scary. Again we don't mess with His words. We don't add to them or we become a cult. We don't take away from them, or we become weak and worldly and so does the name of Jesus in the eyes of a watching world.

For Nourishment

Deuteronomy 8:3 reads, "Man does not live by bread alone but by every word that proceeds from the mouth of God." Through His word, God feeds us like He fed the Hebrews in the desert. Jesus said, "Very truly I tell you, the one who believes has eternal life. I am the bread of life" (John 6:47, 48).

Then He gave them a history lesson. "Your ancestors ate the manna in the wilderness, yet they died" (John 6:49). He was reminding them that when the Hebrews wandered in the desert for forty years God gave them food from heaven. They could in no way provide for themselves, so God was their provision. When they saw His provision on the ground each morning they called it manna (the Hebrew word for "*what is it?*"). The Hebrews ate the manna, and it sustained them each day. Eventually though, they died.

Jesus went on to explain, "But here is the bread that comes down from heaven which anyone may eat and not die. *I Am* the living bread that came down from heaven. Whoever eats this bread will live forever. This bread is my flesh, which I will give for the life of the world" (John 6:50, 51). He then taught them more about His blood and His body. At hearing this message, many of His followers turned away from Him. It is profound that they missed Jesus because they would not "eat" His word.

The prophet Jeremiah hadn't missed it though. He wrote, "Thy words were found and I did eat them, and they were unto me joy and rejoicing in my heart" (Jer. 15:16). The weeping prophet got it. So did Isaiah who wrote, "As the rain and the snow come down from heaven, and do not return to it without watering the earth and making it bud and flourish so that it yields seed for the sower and bread for the eater, so is my word that goes out from my mouth. It will not return empty but will accomplish what I desire and achieve the purpose for which I sent it" (Isaiah 55:10-11). God's word is bread for our souls.

Light my Path

"Thy word is a lamp unto my feet, and a light unto my path"
Psalm 119:105

Thank heavens His word is a lamp unto my feet and a light unto my path for this directionally challenged gal! I have been lost on both sides of the world. I have gotten misplaced in malls, airports, parking lots, cities, and the countryside. While we were on trips or traveling to sporting events when the boys were young, we found ourselves lost in many places in Texas. Then there was one starry night in Cheboksary, Russia . . . I am now hopelessly and gratefully dependent upon my GPS to provide me with the sense that's been missing my entire life. With the GPS application on my phone, not surprisingly, I don't get lost much anymore. When I have clear directions and follow them I seem to get where I am going.

God's word is my map for life, my direction, and my lighthouse. Without it, I am stumbling around in the dark and those around me are following. Hosea 4:6 reads, "My people perish for lack of knowledge." His people, people! That would be us! However, when we begin reading the Bible, we will find it is "for gaining wisdom and instruction; for understanding words of insight; for receiving instruction in prudent behavior, doing what is right, just and fair; for giving prudence to those who are simple (gullible), knowledge and discretion to the young. Let the wise listen and add to their learning, and let the discerning get guidance" (Proverbs 1:1-5).

Look at these verses that open the book of Proverbs. All of this is available to the children of God through His word. These verses are addressed to both the gullible *and* the wise. So whether we think ourselves simple or wise, God tells us that if we want wisdom and direction, ask Him for it. Search it out.

Search out the truth. In Acts 17:11 the Jewish believers in Berea received Paul's message with joy. They would then examine the scriptures every day to see if what Paul said was true. Amen, Bereans! And we should too. They turned to the Lord and read the word for themselves, and He turned on the light in their hearts and showed them His way.

Jesus Leads the Way

Jesus is the Living word, and everything He did was to show *us* the way. He was an obedient son to Joseph and Mary. At twelve He reasoned with the priests in the synagogue in Jerusalem. He showed us the way at His baptism, when led into the desert, and finally in touching and ultimately saving the world. Everywhere He went, every word He spoke, in everything He did Jesus was saying, *follow me*. So who better to emulate than Jesus to see how he used the word of God to win spiritual battles?

In preparation for stepping into the public eye to do the work for which He came, Jesus was led by the Holy Spirit to the desert where He prayed and fasted. The gospels tell us He was led there to be tempted. And He was—for the entire forty days! The deceiver succeeded in tempting Adam and Eve by twisting the words of God ever so little. He gave that a try with Jesus too . . . dumb devil. Of course Jesus countered with what the word really says! Here is Luke's account.

"Jesus, full of the Holy Spirit, left the Jordan and was led by the Spirit into the wilderness, where for forty days he was tempted by the devil. He ate nothing during those days, and at the end of them he was hungry. The devil said to him, "If you are the Son of God, tell this stone to become bread." *Jesus answered, "It is written: 'Man shall not live on bread alone.'"* The devil led him up to a high place and showed him in an instant all the kingdoms of the world. And he said to him, "I will give you all their authority and splendor; it has been given to me, and I can give it to anyone I want to. If you worship me, it will all be yours." *Jesus answered, "It is written: 'Worship the Lord your God and serve him only.'"* The devil led him to Jerusalem and had him stand on the highest point of the temple. "If you are the Son of God," he said, "throw yourself down from here. For it is written, 'He will command his angels concerning you to guard you carefully; they will lift you up in their hands, so that you will not strike your foot against a stone.' Jesus answered, *"It is said: 'Do not put the Lord your God to the test.'"* When the devil had finished all this tempting, he left him until an opportune time (Luke 4:1-15). NIV

Why did Jesus need to be tested and tempted? Because being tempted is being human and Christ was all God *and* all man. He had to undergo the same temptation as all men, and therefore He knows and understands the hurt and temptation of every heart. Again in his suffering and temptation He was showing us the way.

At the end of this time of great trial—a test He passed with flying colors—the Bible tells us He became hungry.

He was tired. He was hungry.

He was right in the middle of God's will.

And He was vulnerable.

We are vulnerable when we listen to the voice of the stranger and step out of God's will, and we are also vulnerable when we are right in the middle of obedience yet weary of the fight. So when do we take a rest from the spiritual fight? When can we let down our guard and stop praying for a season?

Never.

It was in Jesus' weakness and hunger, yet in absolute obedience, that Satan tempted him to cut some corners and compromise. We are tempted in the same way. In a face-to-face encounter with the devil, Jesus, our Shepherd, showed us how to fight with the sword. His reply each time was "It is written" and He quoted the scripture from the Old Testament. Though we are only privy to these last three encounters, I think He had been firing back at the devil's words for forty days with "It is written."

Jesus was in a battle just as Adam and Eve were, but He did not converse with the enemy as did Eve. He responded to the bad dog's twisting words with what the word of God *really* says. That's why we need to know what the word of God really says! Jesus used His meticulously sharpened weapon when answering each of Satan's twisting statements with, "It is written." He was basically saying, "My Daddy says!" Jesus submitted to God by following the Spirit into the desert to be tested for forty days. Then using the word of God, He resisted. And the devil had to flee. Again, the devil doesn't like it when we know who our Daddy is, because when God's kids submit and resist, he has to flee!

"Submit yourselves to God (obey). Resist the devil and he will flee from you" James 4:7

Getting His Word in Me

We see the supernatural *and* practical reasons to have God's word in our heart. But our question may be, "How do I get into His word so His word will get into me? I've tried but I can't seem to find a way that works for me." There are many means to get hold of God's word. Christian book stores are full of Bible study books and aids. You will find a treasure trove of helps there. But before anyone wrote about how to study the Bible, God's people were opening The Book and eating His words.

We can too.

Maybe you don't know much of the Bible. That's OK. We don't have to be Bible scholars to read and understand God's word. We don't have to be Bible scholars to know the depth of His love for us or to turn worry and negative thoughts into prayer and contentment. Each of us at one time started with one verse and one promise. So, one verse at a time begin to follow the Shepherd through your Bible. Here are a few thoughts that might help you navigate your way through His word.

1. Read the gospels, the stories of Jesus's life. Perhaps start with John.

2. Look in the back of your Bible at the concordance. From your concordances, you can dig out the promises of God. Or take a topic like faith, hope, gossip, or repentance and use the concordance to look up scriptures pertaining to that word. Then ask God to show you what He wants you to see.

3. Read a Psalm and a Proverb each day—along with your other study.

4. Read a One-Year Bible or use a study Bible. (My study Bible blesses my heart.)

5. Each time I read my Bible, I date the page or passage where I begin, and God and I chat along the way. I mark things, put question marks alongside verses, and write thoughts to God. I also write the things He is telling me. Or you can use a journal to record the conversations between you and God.

6. I like to mark conjunctions and verbs. Conjunctions at the beginning of a sentence or paragraph point me back or forward. They direct me to look deeper. And verbs show me what God is telling me to do or what He is doing. I ask, "What do you mean here, Lord? What are you talking about?"

7. I mark "I AM" or "I" and the verb that follows any time God is being referenced. Through the entire Bible I can see Who God is and what He is up to. It is powerful, humbling, helpful, hopeful, and beautiful! The "I Am." He's got this, whatever this is!

8. *Not very often,* but occasionally I read the chapter where my Bible has fallen open. Here is an example of what happened when I read the pages that "randomly" opened one night:

I found myself reading from the middle of Daniel when he was asked to interpret the writing on the wall. The writing revealed that that very night the kingdom would fall. By this time Daniel had been a eunuch in Babylon since he was a young man. What I saw over the next few days as I read entire the book is that this man of God was faithful with each day. Whatever his days brought, it did not change his job description that he was to let his life shine **brightly** for God.

As a young man, he was faithful, asking his caregiver to give him only vegetables because the king's food would defile him. He was faithful when serving Nebuchadnezzar who went nuts when God judged his pride. Through Daniel's faithful witness, Nebuchadnezzar repented and came to know the one true God.

Through the remainder of his life Daniel lived faithfully under other wicked kings. As an old man he prayed each day as he always had and ultimately ended up in a den of hungry lions. Though it sounds like a fairy tale, this is history. Daniel stayed the course.

9. Read the word in Context

Most of the time though, I need to read the word in context: the verse in the chapter and the chapter in the book, looking at the time of history it was written, who wrote it, for what purpose it was written and to whom it was written.

The Bible is the greatest history book in the world and is full of beautiful literature. Read one passage. Then read it in context—going to the chapters before and after it. This gives information that helps us understand words and customs that do not make sense to us today. Learning the meanings of words, about the time the text was written, and why the author wrote it will help you understand what you are reading.

The first time I read the book of Joshua, I was a young mother sitting by a window in the early morning light having a sunshine quiet time. Since then I have sat by different windows in different homes in different towns. But even on cloudy days God's sweet Son-Shine is always there.

As I read I saw that Joshua had taken orders from Moses for forty years. Now it was his turn to do God's appointed job. Moses had led them from Egypt. Now Joshua was to lead this army of Hebrews and take the land God promised them. This land was already promised, their possession, sealed by God. But they had to go in and fight for it.

That day, although I was discouraged and sad, God gave me courage. From Joshua, I learned I had to fight for God's gift of peace and contentment. From Joshua, I learned I cannot turn my back on the enemy because the armor God provided does not cover my back. Apathy and complacency in my prayer and time in God's sweet word is turning my back on the enemy. It opens me up for attack. As I sat in the sunshine I learned from Joshua that I can't back up, and I won't give up! He taught me that to win, I had to stay in the fight.

10. Sing the word!

One book of the Bible is a book of songs—the Psalms. David wrote many of them, and his psalms often bring him from despair to peace and joy. The Bible tells us that God inhabits the praises of His children. He moves right into our praises. When He moves in therefore, fear and sorrow move out. One of the most powerful ways to get God's word into our hearts is through song. Songs in the car, songs when you're working, songs when you need encouragement, songs that draw you close to God.

When my boys were little, we learned lots of God's word through song. During a time when our circumstances were particularly lousy, we learned Deuteronomy 32: 3, 4. The chorus was "Ascribe greatness to our God the rock. His work is PERFECT and all His ways are just! A God of faithfulness, without injustice. Righteous and upright is He."

We would sing those words over and over and I would say, "Well, Lord, if your work is perfect and your ways are just and You are a God of faithfulness without injustice . . . we're going to be OK." How can I tell you what these beautiful words meant to us?

These were the words Moses proclaimed before a compromising generation—that God is faithful. And these words have stilled the hearts of three generations of Mays'. I sang to the boys as I sat in the dark hall between their rooms at night. Trent and I sang these words as we lay in the grass with the dogs the week after he graduated from high school. And the next day he was headed to work on an oil rig in the Gulf of

Mexico. It is also the chorus our grandchildren sing at times when I put them to bed.

When Davie was younger she would say, "Gwammy, let's sing 'The Rock'," and she and I and her brother, Brave, sang "The Rock." Rebecca and Brooke sang "The Rock" with me, too. I would sing the low part with my Texas drawl, and they beautifully and in perfect pitch sing the high part.

"The Rock," "Jesus, Jesus, Jesus" and "Lord, You Are More Precious" filled our home as the boys went to sleep at night. From Proverbs we sang, "Lord, you are more precious than silver. Lord you are more costly than gold (Proverbs 3:14). "Lord, you are more beautiful than diamonds. And, nothing I desire compares to You" (from Proverbs 8: 10-11). When we sang those words it put everything into perspective. In those early days I asked myself, "Do you really believe that, Dana?" In those early days I began to learn that, "Life is hard, but yes, yes, I do."

11. Ask others for help to plant the word of God in your heart. What works for them might work for you.

12. Share *your* ideas with others.

13. Look online and use any of the commentaries available. Matthew Henry's is my favorite.

14. Write down the promises.

    "For all the promises of God in Him are Yes, and in Him Amen, to the glory of God through us" (2 Corinthians 1:20). NKJV

They *are*.

Not they were.

There are approximately 7,487 promises in God's sweet word . . . precious promises from God to us. If you have never written down the precepts and promises from God's heart to yours, begin today. It will grow your faith in, trust in, and love for Him. Get some cards, a binder, some paper, or a journal and begin to write down promises. Look on line, or find a book of promises at your book store. Read the promises often and use them when you pray.

His word is true. He is not a liar, and will not fall short of what He says He will do. Our God created the universe and all that was or ever will be. He saved us by ordaining that His perfect Son would be born a babe to a blue collar family in a country with tyranny abounding, and that this Son would grow as a toddler, a child, a teenager, and a young man, perfect in every way. Then this perfect Son revealed Who He was, and for that He was beaten, humiliated, and killed. His death and resurrection brought life to all. We know the promises of God are true. All we have to do is look at Jesus Christ's life, His death, and His resurrection.

Start Today

We may know very little of God's word. Or we might have learned some of His truth at one time but have misplaced it in the recesses of our heart. I challenge you to start today, to pull those truths out, dust them off, and begin believing them again. Or perhaps you have never memorized a single verse.

Begin today, one promise and precept at a time, replacing the lies of the world with God's beautiful truth. Then when the enemy pours hopeless, twisted, or evil thoughts through your mind, listen instead for the Shepherd and tell him, "Wait a minute buster! This is what my Daddy says!" When I open my door in the afternoon, the darkness does not move onto the porch. The light pours in from outside and fills up the room. Light overtakes darkness. The sword of the Spirit, God's mighty word, offensively pushes back the darkness and ushers God's light into our hearts and the world around us.

The word of God is a weapon against the enemy of our souls. But most importantly, it is the way to a loving relationship with our Shepherd, Jesus Christ. God will not critique our method as we pursue this relationship, but He wants us to show up to the table often to eat the Bread of Life, to speak to Him, and to listen for His voice. That's how relationship grows. For that reason there is perhaps no battle the devil wants to win more than the battle to keep you and me out of the Book and away from sincere relationship with God.

Satan doesn't mind ethereal prayer or lofty words. He doesn't even mind us dutifully having our quiet time and checking it off as done. He wants to keep us at arm's length from God though. His greatest threat is our authentic conversation with God as we read His words and talk with Him about *everything,* you know, because He's our Daddy. When we break through that barrier to authenticity, the devil has lost us to God. He has lost his ability to scare the daylights out of us, and lost the time he can swim around in our thoughts and take us on a wild goose chase.

Intimacy with God.

Sweet familiarity with the voice of the Shepherd.

It's worth fighting for.

Learning the Secret

Below are a few promises that I have held onto which continue to change my heart day by day and give me contentment. In this lesson are examples of praying God's words, His promises. Write out the scriptures below. These promises are yours.

1. Isaiah 55: 10,11:

That is powerful! Your word will accomplish what You have intended. It's a promise to me! I cannot tell you the times I have felt hopeless in my prayer, but His promise is true!

A	D	M	F	M	N	D
T	N	I	T	W	R	A
R	R	B	S	T	T	A
A	T	A	A	G	M	T
S	I	F,	B	O	E,	P
C	W	S	F	O	B	F
D	W	T	T	M	W	W
F	T	I	E,	M:	A	I
H	E	Y	S	I	W	S
A	A	S	I	W	I	I.

2. 2 Timothy 1:7:

This sick fear in my gut, the frenzied panic, or need to control every outcome is not from God. It is a destructive delivery from Satan. God's gift is His power, and love pouring in and through me, and a sound mind—yes, a firm, reliable, sensible mind! Say it out loud. Mull it over in your brain. Fight!

F	G	O	P	A	M.
G	U	F,	A	O	
H	A	B	O	A	
N	S	O	L	S	

_____

_____

3. John 14:27:

Jesus left this gift for me and my family. The Prince of Peace died and rose and left me His peace. It is mine.

P	M	I	Y	D	B	B
I	P	D	A	N	T	A.
L	I	N	T	L	A	
W	G	G	W	Y	D	
Y	Y.	T	G.	H	N	

_____

_____

4. Philippians 1:6:

Oh, it seems impossible. Thank you, Lord, that You will complete the work You have begun in me and my beloved family!

B	T	A	Y	O	T	J.
C	H	G	W	T	D	
O	W	W	C	C	O	
T	B	I	I	U	C	

_____

_____

5. Romans 8:28, 29:

All things, even the mess we might find ourselves in? Yes. Thank you, God, that You are weaving even these things into the tapestry of our lives to use us to Your glory, to change me, to help others, and bring to them to Christ.

A	G	T	G	L	W	T
W	C	W	T	G,	A	H
K	A	T	T	T	C	P.
T	T	F	W	T	A	(NASB)

_____

_____

6. Psalm 118:29:

Thank you for your love and mercy, Lord. Thank you that you will love us forever and ever and ever.

G	T	H	H	F.
T	L	I	L	
T	F	G.	E	

_____

_____

7. Joel 2:25a:

You see what I and others have made of my life. Do you really mean you can make it new? Can you forgive me and fix me? I believe that is exactly what you mean. When I am sad and beyond discouraged I will hold onto this promise that you will restore, make brand new, all that has been robbed from us.

| I | W | R | Y | F | T | Y | T | L |
| | H | E | | | | | | |

_____

_____

8. Proverbs 3:5,6:

Lord, I want to trust You with everything in me. But, this is a scary time, such a hurtful time! I trust you, Lord. Help my shaky knees. I can't figure this out, so I won't try. I am going to acknowledge You in all this, and know somehow, someway, You are going to take this crooked path and straighten it out.

T		W	A	Y	A	T	W	S.
I		A	L	O	Y	H	M	
T		Y	N	U;	W	A	Y	
L		H	O	I	S	H	P	

---

9. Isaiah 26:3:

I must keep my eyes and heart on You, Lord? "Yes, Dana, keep your eyes and heart on Me, and I will draw your heart and mind back to Me."

Y		I	M	Y,	I
W		P	I	B	Y.
K		P	S	H	
H		W	0	T	(NKJV)

---

10. Isaiah 54:17a:

Ok, beloved Father, this is a good one. Do you mean that I can actually ask you to divert the fiery darts aimed at me and my family and you will hear me? I am going to say this in my brain, mull it over, and believe it!

N   W   F   A   Y   W   P

_____

_____

11. Psalm 118:24:

You made this day, dear Lord, I will be glad in it, I will, by Your grace in me, rejoice.

T	T	W	B
I	L	W	G
T	H	R	I
D	M.	A	I. (NKJV)

_____

_____

12. 1 Timothy 6:6,7:

Godliness and contentment in You, Lord, is great gain. Thank you Lord.

B	I	W	T	T	I
G	G	B	W	N	
W	G.	N	A	O	
C	F	I	C	O	

Thank you, Lord, for today. I choose to be content in and thankful for all you have given me, Lord. Nothing, nothing, nothing I desire compares to You.

In Jesus precious name.
Amen

Part 3
Talking with the Shepherd

8

PRAY without Ceasing
(Right Out Loud)

Why has God summoned us to pray if He is the Sovereign God who already knows the beginning of time to the end? Prayer is about our relationship with God and is for His glory. It is the way He has set up His kingdom. Prayer builds a relationship with God that glorifies Him and blesses and empowers us. He is our Father. We are His children created for a relationship that will mold us into His image so our lives will touch our world.

An investment of time is what builds a relationship. The better we know someone the more we trust them. Our prayer is simply talking with and staying in touch with our Father and getting to know Him. It is listening for His voice knowing that nothing of real value can be accomplished apart from prayer. It gives me joy when I see Granddad (Don) or my big ol' sons or sons-in-law stoop down and scoop up one of the grandchildren to hold in their arms. I see such delight in those daddy, granddad, and uncle eyes when the kids reach back to them.

In describing God's love, David said: "*You stoop down to make me great.*" (Psalm 18:35b). Jesus stooped down when he was born in a stable in Bethlehem. He stooped down to live among a bunch of sinners for thirty-three years. He stooped down to reveal the religious folk's hypocrisy and to forgive Mary Magdalene's sins. He stooped down to ask the woman at the well in Samaria for water so she could receive the Living Water. He stooped down as

He was being rejected for speaking The Truth. He stooped down as He was forsaken by those closest to Him. And He stooped down to me as he spread His arms and allowed Himself to be nailed to a cross. When we talk to God and read His love letter, we are reaching our arms and hearts back to Him.

Pray Continually

Remember that Paul's final instructions to the Thessalonians included three imperatives. "Rejoice always, pray continually, and give thanks in all circumstances; for this is God's will for you in Christ Jesus" (1 Thessalonians 5:16-18). Notice that this verse says pray *continually*.

So how do we pray continually? How do we grow our relationship with our Father in Heaven to such a degree that we are talking to Him much of the time? How do we guard against compartmentalizing our relationship with Him into quiet time, church time, Bible study time, and the rest of the time? How can we become people who don't just talk about prayer, but pray?

When our son was on a flight before his first deployment to Iraq, he sat next to an officer who was returning from combat. As they talked, he realized this man was a believer. Knowing our son, a young combat officer himself, was soon heading to war, this brother's parting advice was, "Pray as you go, son. Pray as you go." This officer had learned what it is to pray continually. He knew he could not walk out his duties each day without God unless he prayed without ceasing.

Prayer-Walkin'

I often pray God's words when I am praying for my family and the world so when I walk in the neighborhood I take my scripture journal with me to memorize and pray. The neighbors think I am a crazy woman as I walk and pray God's sweet words right out loud, but that's OK. I won't stop. When we are frightened, discouraged, broken-hearted, worried, or weary we might not have the words to pray. We have God's words though.

So slathering sunscreen on my face, pulling on my hat, and clutching my book of verses, I head out the back door. Around the house and onto the asphalt I feel the hot road pulsing like a furnace on my face. I smell the heat. The locust song is a deafening serenade reverberating from one clump of trees to another. Melodious clicks from the grass hoppers jumping out of the way of my feet are evidence it's almost August in Texas. I turn the corner heading north and feel the faintest hint of relief from the heat.

At a time that I was desperate and looking to God for help, a friend gave me a copy of Stormie Omartian's *Power of a Praying Wife*. I loved that book and every book on prayer Stormie has written. I had been praying for a long time, but this is when my prayer-walkin' days began.

Prayer walking encompasses two things: praying and walking.

The walking part is obedience. I am not a physical kind of girl. God put my soul in this body though. It's the wrapping paper. So, I struggle to eat right and walk to take care of the wrapping that's holding the gift inside.

I struggle.

This hot day in July I am walking but haven't started talking to God yet.

He's talking to me though. In the trees and in the locusts' clicks, God is talking to me. In the three tomatoes that are growing from the many blooms on my tomato plants, God is talking to me. In the brilliant blue sky and bellowing clouds, even in the heat of the pavement, and sweet relief when I turn the corner to go north, He is talking to me.

I turn onto the next street. I come to a yellow house. I start talking to Him.

The walking part is obedience; the prayer part is love. It's a longing in my heart to have one more conversation with my Savior, the One who created me and loves me completely.

The One who always hears the cry of my heart.

Lord, please wrap your arms around this precious family. Their hearts are broken. Their son fought on the other side of the world in two wars and came home only to die of an overdose of prescription drugs.

That little house at the end of the street is loved. You can tell there was great thought in the way they planned and planted. *But this family is gone, Lord.* I have no idea what happened: death, divorce, job change, or calamity. They just left.

I keep walking.

The house on the next corner is shaded by beautiful trees. This gal has two dogs and two sons—teenagers. Dad died when they were little boys. She's raised them alone for a long time. *They are going through rough times, Father. Help them.*

This next house is the prettiest in the neighborhood and the biggest. *Lord, you know the charming lady who lives here. She lives alone, has plenty of money, a great job, and a cool car. But, Lord, she is so alone.*

I keep walking.

I look at the journal of verses tucked under my arm . . . my Bread of Life. I read the beautiful words of God and pray them back to Him. There couldn't be better words to pray for myself, my beloved husband, or for my family so precious to me. No better words to pray for this neighborhood in this sleepy town in Texas as I cry out to God in their behalf. No better words to pray for a hurting world.

Praying—that's what I can do. What I must do. What I am blessed to do. My heart touching His—crying out for a hurting world. This is a little praying without ceasing and one more conversation with the God who loves me completely.

Help Me Jesus Prayer

A young woman told me she did not know how to pray and would never pray out loud. I understand that fear, but it is unfounded. We are God's children, and a good Father loves his children's words. Perhaps some of the dearest words I have ever heard were those of my children and grandchildren as they were learning to talk. The first "Mama," "Meme" or "Gammy" were precious. And the sentences I had to listen to carefully to understand were love to my heart. Our communications with our Father in Heaven are dear to His heart in the same way.

Our sons and sons in law pray with and for their children. One of our sons is a seminary graduate and can utter some pretty lofty prayers. He doesn't though. His out loud prayers with his family are sweet and simple. Lofty prayers are not what God requires, but He listens to the humble hearts of His children seeking to communicate with Him.

There are about 650 prayers recorded in the Bible and they represent a plethora more. Most are from ordinary people like you and me who are crying out to God. From them, we learn that prayer does not have to be perfect. From them, we see that our prayers will continue to change and grow as our relationship with our Heavenly Father grows. Our most powerful prayers can be as simple as, "Help me, Jesus."

God hears.

God answers.

Help Me Jesus

The year I became a believer I was attending night classes for my master's degree in administration. I'm not sure I'm an administrator by any reach, but there I was. The class was small, perhaps ten or twelve students. I realized everyone in the class was serving in administrative positions except me. A lowly fourth grade teacher trying to do the job I had, I was in the middle of a wide learning curve. I couldn't see a thing ahead.

Because I was a classroom teacher, I had no stories or daily dilemmas to contribute to the class discussion. I furiously took notes and kept my mouth shut the entire semester. I made it to the end and to the last twenty minutes comprising the largest percentage of our grade. We were to present an old school power point presentation on an assigned topic. I thought to myself, *I write lesson plans, grade papers, teach multiplication, division, world history, and language skills. And I have to stand in front of administrators and convince them that I know what I am talking about?* I was mortified as I listened to the other presentations. I prayed like a child, "Help me Jesus. I can't do this. Help me Jesus."

My turn came. The room was dark except for the light shining on the material I was presenting *and* on my face. In my heart still uttering the "Help me Jesus" prayer I began—hoping no one could see me sweating. I have no idea what I said. It was one of those surgery-like experiences where you remember going to sleep and waking up but nothing in between.

The professor made comments for the other presenters as soon as they finished. But after I finished, there was silence in the room. I am sure it was for less than a minute but it seemed like an eternity. Then from the back of the dark room came the words, "*You* are a sleeper!" I widened my eyes and looked out into the darkness. "You are a sleeper, Mrs. Mays." he repeated. "You have been sitting here for the entire semester and have not said a word. This presentation was excellent. You should be in public relations in the business world." I smiled and thanked him. As I gathered my things and sat down I thought to myself. *I am in public relations— in my classroom every day—for Jesus.*

Only months before, my world had been turned upside down by this Jesus to whom I had called out. Only a few months later I, a new mommy, would be sitting on my porch crying and uttering the same prayer. I am *still* doing public relations work for Jesus and I have called out "Help me Jesus" thousands of times since then. Praying without ceasing is simply calling out to God for help.

The Name

Calling out to God in Jesus' name, that's what we do. He is Creator God *and* Savior of the world. As my granddaughter, Brooke, emphatically announced when she was three years old, "Grammy, Jesus is God!" Yes, Jesus is the One True God. Though Jesus was a common name in Judea in the first century, it is the Name Above all Names. How like God to give His Son, the Savior of the world, a common name. Again, He stooped down.

In ancient civilizations and in some cultures today, the word of the king is the final word. The mark of the king seals every deal—lending it authenticity, power, and authority. It was Jesus, the King who said, "Until now you have not asked for anything in my name. Ask and you will receive, and your joy will be complete" (John 16: 24). He gave these specific instructions to his disciples the night of His betrayal. Praying in Jesus name acknowledges that we can do nothing apart from Him.

The disciples heard what Jesus said that night—that they were to utter their prayers in His name. After Jesus' resurrection and the coming of the Holy Spirit at Pentecost, a man crippled from birth was healed, and Peter proclaimed to those watching, ". . . it is the name of Jesus which has strengthened this man whom you see and know" (Acts 3:16b).

We can pray a lot of things a lot of ways, but it is the beautiful name of Jesus of Nazareth, the Christ, that ushers our prayer into the very presence of God. We don't have to shout it, and we don't have to repeat it a thousand times. We merely mention the powerful name. Then God the Father, recognizing the blood of Jesus that has washed us as white as snow, sees Jesus. In us He sees Jesus and replies, "What can I do for you, child?"

> Jesus, Jesus, Jesus, there is something about that name.
> Jesus, Jesus, Jesus like the fragrance after the rain.
> Jesus, Jesus, Jesus let all Heaven and earth proclaim.
> Kings and kingdoms will all pass away, *(but not Jesus)*
> Because there is something about that name!
> (Bill & Gloria Gaither)

There definitely is something about that name!

Right Out Loud

The Bible is full of out loud praying. In the Old Testament, Abraham, Moses, Daniel, Elijah, Elisha, Isaiah, and Jeremiah to name a few prayed right out loud. In the New Testament we witness the out loud prayers of God's children, as well. But the out loud prayers I love most are Jesus' prayers. We know He was a praying without-ceasing-man. And because He was, eye witnesses could later write some of His prayers down for us.

Learning the Secret

Jesus Prays for Himself

"Knowing he was going to be betrayed and leave His beloved disciples, He taught them continually. They had eaten the Passover meal, He had washed their feet, He had taught them about The Holy Spirit, about abiding in Him, and about the persecution that would come. They had not yet crossed the valley and gone over to Gethsemane, that familiar spot where they had prayed many times before.

It is then that John writes: "He looked up to Heaven and prayed. 'Father, the hour has come. Glorify your Son, that your Son may glorify you. For you granted him authority over all people that he might give eternal life to all those you have given him. Now this is eternal life: that they know you, the only true God, and Jesus Christ, whom you have sent. I have brought you glory on earth by finishing the work you gave me to do. And now, Father, glorify me in your presence with the glory I had with you before the world began'" (John 17:1-5).

What did Jesus reveal in His prayer for Himself?

_____

_____

Jesus Prays for His Disciples

"I have revealed you to those whom you gave me out of the world. They were yours; you gave them to me and they have obeyed your word. Now they know that everything you have given me comes from you. For I gave them the words you gave me and they accepted them. They knew with certainty that I came from you, and they believed that you sent me. I pray for them. I am not praying for the world, but for those you have given me, for they are yours. All I have is yours, and all you have is mine. And glory has come to me through them. I will remain in the world no longer, but they are still in the world, and I am coming to you. Holy Father, protect them by the power of your name, the name you gave me, so that they may be one as we are one. While I was with them, I protected them and kept them safe by that name you gave me. None has been lost except the one doomed to destruction so that Scripture would be fulfilled. "I am coming to you now, but I say these things while I am still in the world, so that they may have the full measure of my joy within them. I have given them your word and the world has hated them, for they are not of the world any more than I am of the world. My prayer is not that you take them out of the world but that you protect them from the evil one. They are not of the world, even as I am not of it. Sanctify them by the truth; your word is truth. As you sent me into the world, I have sent them into the world. For them I sanctify myself, that they too may be truly sanctified" (John 17:6-19).

What did He say about His disciples and what did He pray for them?

_____

_____

Jesus Prays for All Believers

"My prayer is not for them alone. I pray also for those who will believe in me through their message, that all of them may be one, Father, just as you are in me and I am in you. May they also be in us so that the world may believe that you have sent me. I have given them the glory that you gave me, that they may be one as we are one—I in them and you in me—so that they may be brought to complete unity. Then the world will know that you sent me and have loved them even as you have loved me. "Father, I want those you have given me to be with me where I am, and to see my glory, the glory you have given me because you loved me before the creation of the world ."Righteous Father, though the world does not know you, I know you, and they know that you have sent me. I have made you known to them, and will continue to make you known in order that the love you have for me may be in them and that I myself may be in them" (John 17:20-26).

What did He say about us and pray for us?

_____

_____

How can I apply the focus of Christ's prayer to my prayer life?

_____

_____

.

9

Pray Without Ceasing
(In Your Closet)

Jesus had many prayer closets. His prayer closet (His war room) was wherever He went by himself to pray. And he prayed often. Ephesians 6:18 reads ". . . with the Sword of the Spirit, which is the word of God . . . pray in the Spirit on all occasions, with all kinds of prayers and requests. With this in mind, be alert and always keep on praying for all the saints."

We looked at Chapter 6 of Ephesians to see God's battle plan for the spiritual fight. It is not coincidental that Paul gives us a how-to for unity in the body of Christ in Ephesians 4 and specifics for the Christian family in Ephesians 5 and 6. It is then followed by instructions on how to fight the spiritual battle. The order of that admonition and the instructions on how to fight are not coincidental. The enemy continually fights against unity in the body of Christ and against the Christian family.

So what does this family seeking contentment in Christ look like? The call is for wives to submit to husbands. That's a novel idea. It is for husbands to lead and love their wives like Christ gave Himself for the church. Again this is rare in our culture. It is for children to honor and obey their parents, for fathers (and mothers) not to provoke their children to anger, and to lead them to the Lord. Sadly, these attributes are perhaps rarest of all. Order, respect, protection, and unity are all God stuff, counter to our culture and to our nature. Yet we have a gentle Shepherd whose voice beckons us to this life, through a sweet, relationship with Him. And even with our warts and scars this makes for a family that has the aroma of Christ.

I ask mommas who are having problems with their kids, "How are you praying for your children?" Many times they look at me with a blank stare and have no real answer. The fact is, a lot of us in the body of Christ do not pray much or at all. When we do, we are often too impatient to wait for God's answers or surprised when He does answer.

No doubt as emotions and circumstances lead, we may anxiously bat at the air not even knowing how to pray. As we are learning though, that is when we decide whose voice we are going to listen to. That is when we turn our thoughts to God and what His words say. We can't live this life of grace without prayer, and takes a lot of prayer! The more we wield the sword of the Spirit and pray, the more our public life and private life will be the same. (What a relief!)

For this battle, we pray right out loud *and* we pray in our closets.

Closet Prayer (Our War Room)

Some of the religious men in the first century uttered loud and lofty prayers so everyone could see how holy they were and marvel at the eloquence of their pronouncements to God. If they prayed so folks could see them, folks saw them. Jesus told them they had their reward in full. That was all they would receive. Some pray primarily to be heard by others.

Jesus showed us though that prayer is preparation for everything. From prayers come supernatural answers from the throne of grace. He taught us, "But when you pray, go into your room, close the door and pray to your Father, who is unseen. Then your Father, who sees what is done in secret, will reward you" (Matthew 6:6).

Observing the hypocrisy in the Jewish priest's public prayers, He told us to go into our closet to pray; to go to a private place to call out to God. He showed us what that looks like when throughout the gospels Jesus went out by Himself to pray. Gethsemane, where He often prayed when He was in Jerusalem, was just one of Jesus' prayer closets.

As the movie depicts, our prayer closet is our War Room. It is there that we do battle. My sitting still prayer closet from the time I began praying and reading the Bible is by a window, any window where God's sweet light shines through. My prayer is not only by a sunny window though. Our war room can be in the car, a hall, a favorite chair, or under a tree. It is wherever we are. Remember the parting advice my son received from the officer? "Pray as you go, son. Pray as you go."

We battle in bed, sitting in traffic, walking, shopping, at work, at home, in a crowd, or all alone. Regular alone time with God, we all need it. So did Jesus. He prayed right out loud for Himself, for the disciples, and for us. But He knew He needed more time with His Father in order to courageously go to the cross. Look at the precious nuggets of truth in Jesus' prayer at Gethsemane.

It reads: "Then Jesus went with his disciples to a place called Gethsemane, and he said to them, 'Sit here while I go over there and pray.' He took Peter and the two sons of Zebedee along with him, and he began to be sorrowful and troubled. Then he said to them, 'My soul is overwhelmed with sorrow to the point of death. Stay here and keep watch with me.'

Going a little farther, he fell with his face to the ground and prayed, 'My Father, if it is possible, may this cup be taken from me. Yet not as I will, but as you will.' Then he returned to his disciples and found them sleeping. 'Couldn't you men keep watch with me for one hour?' he asked Peter. 'Watch and pray so that you will not fall into temptation. The spirit is willing, but the flesh is weak.

'He went away a second time and prayed, 'My Father, if it is not possible for this cup to be taken away unless I drink it, may your will be done.' When he came back, he again found them sleeping, because their eyes were heavy. So he left them and went away once more and prayed the third time, saying the same thing. Then he returned to the disciples and said to them, 'Are you still sleeping and resting? Look, the hour has come, and the Son of Man is delivered into the hands of sinners. Rise! Let us go! Here comes my betrayer!'" (Matthew 26:36-46). Jesus went back to His war room again and again until he prayed away the fear and could courageously walk out His purpose in God's will.

Two gardens.

One at the beginning and one at the end.

God shed the blood of an animal (perhaps a lamb) to cover Adam and Eve in Eden, and they fled from the Garden in shame and nakedness. Now the Lamb of God is praying in Gethsemane, and only hours later would give His life's blood to cover the sin of the whole world.

Contentious times.

He knew what that night and the next day would require of Him. He knew He could not endure it without His Father's help. So He went to his knees in prayer, and He summoned the prayers of his beloved disciples. Though they were weak and continued to fall asleep, Jesus prayed. He went to the secret place of the Most High with such fervent prayer that His sweat was like blood. How like God to show us in His most desperate moment His most complete prayer.

He knew how desperately He and his friends needed to pray as fear and dread at taking the sins of the world on Himself washed over Him. Yet each time He went to His disciples they were asleep. He exhorted them, " . . . Watch and pray so that you will not fall into temptation. The spirit is willing, but the flesh is weak" (Matthew 26:41). He knew He was weak of spirit and desperately needing the intercessory prayers of His beloved ones. He also knew that unless they were watching and praying they *would* fall into temptation, and that is exactly what happened.

In the Lord's out loud prayer (Lord's Prayer) Jesus prayed to the Father. "Lead us not into temptation, but deliver us from evil." And in His last prayer in the garden before He was led off to be crucified He exhorted the disciples to pray so they would not fall into temptation. Jesus knew their flesh was weak, and so is ours. But He gave us the remedy. "Watch and pray so you will not fall into temptation." The way we avoid temptation (those ditches the enemy puts in front of us to fall into again and again) is to set our mind on things above and to *pray*!

Should we not follow the Shepherd in this? Yes, for ourselves and those for whom we pray, ask that we will not be led into temptation. Because if we're not praying, the pirates are at the helm! When we set our minds on things above through prayer though, the voice of the good dog gets louder and sweeter. The voice of the bad dog diminishes.

Closet praying, wherever it is, and spending time with God is what changes us. Moments of sitting, walking, being quiet, sharing our heart, voicing our fears and concerns like Abraham, Moses, David, and Paul did, change us. Reading His words, listening for His voice, and spending time with Him changes us from the inside out. Changes we can see and so can the faces in front of us.

When I read in Exodus that Moses spent forty days and nights with God on the mountain I noticed a few things. He didn't have anything to eat or drink. Can you imagine eating no food for forty days? Yet he wasn't hungry or thirsty. He had been heart to heart, listening for the voice of God, and time with God has a way of quieting our flesh. It just does.

When Moses came down from his intimate, uninterrupted, honest, deep time with God, his face was changed. "When Moses came down from Mount Sinai with the two tablets of the covenant law in his hands, he was not aware that his face was radiant because he had been speaking with the Lord" (Exodus 34:29). Moses' face was radiant!

The more time we spend with God, the more we love and trust Him. The more we know Him, the less we are going to worry about circumstances. The more we know Him, the more content we are with where He has us. The more we know Him, the less we are going to care what people think. The more we know Him, the more we have the ultimate *yes* face. It's a face that glows from deep inside. It is a supernatural radiance that we, our family, and our world are desperate for.

Mind Setting Prayer

I used to step into church worried about whether I was all put together, dress zipped, hair smooth, tags hidden, and lookin' good. I still don't like those bad hair days, but some time ago, I realized it wasn't about me. I needed to set my mind on things above. Paul wrote to the Colossians, "Set your mind on things above, not on the things of the earth" (Colossians 3:2). "To set" means to take an action with deliberate purpose. Prayer and speaking those things that God says are true, sets my mind on God things. Things above probably have very little to do with my bad hair day and all to do with people.

The people around me.

The souls of men.

Now as I ease into my seat next to my husband before the service begins, I observe the people around me, and I pray for them. I invite the Holy Spirit in asking Him to touch hearts. I pray for a husband and wife because the tension between them is palpable. I pray for the little wife who longs for her husband's attention, or the husband who is totally beaten down by the woman sitting next to him. I pray for those who are obviously uncomfortable in church and perhaps hearing the gospel for the first time. I pray for our pastor as he teaches. Though my bad hair days have preoccupied my thoughts at times, it's not about me. It's about the souls of men, so one of our prayer closets is the church pew.

United In Prayer

Jesus asked his disciples to join Him in prayer because there is power in numbers. We are a body and we need each other. "Though one may be overpowered, two can defend themselves. A cord of three strands is not quickly broken" (Ecclesiastes 4:12). Me, another believer, and Jesus. That is power! We pray with and for one another sharing our burdens with each other. Praying for one another is like handing off bags of heavy groceries and allowing our brothers and sisters in Christ to help us with the load.

Of course, the most powerful prayer team in the world is a believing husband and wife. That's why the devil hates marriage and is in full attack mode to destroy marriage and family. For years I didn't have a husband to pray with. I was so busy teaching school and raising children that I didn't have time to invest in friendships other than my co-teachers. We were believers and we did pray together, but my primary prayer partners in those years were my children. During those times, my boys and I would join hands, join hearts, and pray!

When you are struggling and need help, call someone to pray with you and for you. Ask, "Could you meet with me, pray with me on the phone, or pray for me?" Don't give up. Keep looking until you find someone with skin on to pray with. Whether you realize it or not though, Someone is always praying for you. Jesus, your Shepherd is interceding for you before the Father. He is calling your name out to God.

Jesus is praying for us. When the stranger accuses us, He stands in our defense. "Therefore He is able also to save forever those who draw near to God through Him, since He always lives to make intercession for us" (Hebrews 7:25). He is bridging the gap between us and the Father. There is such comfort in knowing that Jesus is praying for us, defending us, and bridging that gap.

We pray out loud. We pray in our closet. We pray with others in the body of Christ. We are being prayed for by Jesus Christ, our Shepherd. And all prayer is sweet communication between the Father and His children.

Because the fervent prayer of a righteous man avails much, we practice prayer.

Practice Prayer

Remember Daniel who prayed every day through every season of his life? Like Jesus he was a man of persistent prayer. To be persistent in prayer though, takes commitment *and* practice. I learned a lesson about how to practice makes perfect through Max, a short grumpy dog with barbeque sauce colored whiskers. Max was the last of a passel of dogs the boys grew up with. When Max was a puppy Parker called him Mickey. Trent called him Max. So perhaps he was neurotic. For whatever reason though, Max was a stinker.

A gift from a neighbor, he was delivered to our back door in a little basket. The minute he arrived, he displaced our sweet puppy, Millie, as the alpha dog. Even though he never bit anyone, if we got inside his comfort zone, he would utter a growl that warned us to back off.

He was one disagreeable dog.

Years moved into more than a decade and I often referred to him as butt-cuss, because he was. One summer after the boys went to college, Kristi, who would later become Chris' wife, entered our lives. Kristi made Max her special project. She slept with him, talked to him, and she practiced with ol' butt-cuss.

She would look in his eyes and say, "Let's practice being sweet, Muxie." She would move closer, and he would growl. Kristi would whisper sweet nothings in his ear, and move a little closer. As the summer drew to a close, he growled less and less. Finally that grumpy dog loved and trusted Kristi so much that he quit growling. They practiced and practiced until Muxie was sweet.

Practice at anything makes us good at it. The more we talk to our Father in Heaven the more comfortable we are in talking with Him. So, what are we practicing? Remember the Chinese proverb? The good dog, the gentle voice of the Shepherd gives us peace, courage, hope, warning, direction, wisdom, and perspective. His voice draws us to pray. So we practice our faith, turning a habit of worry, fear, bitterness, sorrow, and anxiety into words of prayer. We turn our thoughts of people, concerns of tomorrow, and sorrows over yesterday into prayer releasing it all to Him.

Surrendered Prayer

Prayers of surrender.

The ultimate prayer of surrender, of course, was Christ saying to the Father, 'Not my will but Thine,' before he was nailed to the cross. We will all ultimately surrender to God - either on this side of eternity or the next. Prayers of surrender are sweet and freeing. They are prayers that say, "I have no idea what You are doing, Lord, or how this thing is going to turn out. Even though it scares me not knowing what in the world is around this curve ahead, I'll do it any way you want me to. I give it to you."

Isaac's son, Jacob, had trouble doing things God's way. Because he had trouble with God, He had trouble with people his entire life. His name, in fact, means usurper. A usurper is one who seizes and holds by force. Jacob always seemed to have an angle; he did things to get his way. It started early. When he came out of his mother's womb he was holding onto his twin brother's heel. After a lifetime of relationship problems, immerging from a wrestling match with The Angel of God with a dislocated hip and a new name, Jacob had *finally* surrendered to God. The limp he carried from perhaps that night on reminded Jacob, now named Israel, that he didn't have to go through life with an angle. It reminded him that he could trust and be content with God's plan for his life. For a great read, the story of Jacob's life is in Genesis 25-47.

Look at the apostle Paul and how God got his attention so he would follow Him to do the work for which He was called. A man of principle and excellence, no one was more fervent at going after those blaspheming followers of Christ than Paul before his conversion. He could not find contentment unless every 'i' was dotted and every 't' was crossed.

While traveling to arrest more Christians, God blinded him. This persecutor of believers lay in a bed in Damascus totally blind—unable to see one step in front of him. That is when he realized he didn't need to see what was out front. All he needed to do was to keep his eyes on the feet of the Shepherd, stay in his shadow, and listen for His voice. And God used this man with a determined temperament to teach us about being content.

In blinding Paul, God stopped him in his tracks and eliminated every distraction that had prevented him from hearing His voice. There stood Jesus before him asking him, "Saul, why are you persecuting Me?" At that moment he was radically converted to Christ. And through his writings he taught us that he had, ". . . learned the secret of being content in *all* circumstances" (Philippians 4:12).

Surrender.

Surrender in war brings peace, and surrender to God brings peace . . . and contentment.

Our surrender is to our Shepherd, our Father. Our prayer signifies surrender to Almighty God. When I am on my knees, what can I do? How much work can I get done? What tasks can I accomplish? What opinion can I offer? When I am in a posture of prayer, I can do nothing. If there is any doing, God must do it. Jesus surrendered to the Father and saved the world. Jacob surrendered to the Father and became Israel, in the linage of Jesus. Paul surrendered to God and in doing His work found contentment.

I will, as well. When I surrender all to Him, I follow the Shepherd even though I don't know where He is taking me. I walk in a peace and contentment that the world does not understand, because in the midst of this helplessness and surrender before a Holy God the battle is His. "Prayer throws faith on God and God on the world. Only God can move mountains, but faith and prayer move God" (E.M. Bounds).

Reach up and grab God's hand that is lovingly extended down to you, open your Bibles and pray, listening for the voice of God. "It is here a broken heart rises filled with forgiveness. It is here strongholds are broken. It is here impossible sorrows turn into strength for the day. It is here we find hopes and miracles for tomorrow as the Bread of Life, His matchless word, through our prayers moves the very hand of God" (*Prayer and Spiritual Warfare;* E.M. Bounds, p.8). Amen!

> I have a treasure which I prize. Its like I cannot find.
> There's nothing like it on the earth—'Tis this, a quiet mind.

(Unknown author;
Streams in the Desert, vol. 2)

A quiet mind . . . worth fighting for.

Sweet Father in Heaven, we pray that we and those we love will listen for the voice of the Shepherd and recognize the nagging voice of fear, doubt, need to control, jealousy, and discontentment as the evil voice of a stranger. Still that voice, Father, in Jesus' name! Help us to listen to and believe the voice of our beautiful Shepherd. He's the One who gives us the power, love and sound mind to do whatever is on our plate. To raise the children He has given us, thrive in the difficult circumstances, jobs, and marriages He has given us, to beat substance abuse, heal from abusive backgrounds and broken hearts, and love a hurting world. May we know your voice so well, Lord, that when we hear the stranger we recognize it and we run to You. Help us to do what we can do and leave the rest to You - and help us to know the difference.

In Jesus' Beautiful Name,
Amen

Learning the Secret

1. "Therefore confess your sins to each other and pray for each other so that you may be healed. The prayer of a righteous person is powerful and effective" (James 5:16).

   Confession → Prayer → Healing → powerful and effective prayer

   What is Jesus' little brother, James, telling us in this verse?

   _____

   _____

   _____

   _____

2. Look again at the scene at Gethsemane in Matthew 26:36-46. Then answer the question below: Then Jesus went with his disciples to a place called Gethsemane, and he said to them, "Sit here while I go over there and pray." He took Peter and the two sons of Zebedee along with him, and he began to be sorrowful and troubled. Then he said to them, "My soul is overwhelmed with sorrow to the point of death. Stay here and keep watch with me." Going a little farther, he fell with his face to the ground and prayed, "My Father, if it is possible, may this cup be taken from me. Yet not as I will, but as you will." Then he returned to his disciples and found them sleeping. "Couldn't you men keep watch with me for one

hour?" he asked Peter. "Watch and pray so that you will not fall into temptation. The spirit is willing, but the flesh is weak." He went away a second time and prayed, "My Father, if it is not possible for this cup to be taken away unless I drink it, may your will be done." When he came back, he again found them sleeping, because their eyes were heavy. So he left them and went away once more and prayed the third time, saying the same thing. Then he returned to the disciples and said to them, "Are you still sleeping and resting? Look, the hour has come, and the Son of Man is delivered into the hands of sinners. Rise! Let us go! Here comes my betrayer!

What happened at Gethsemane? Break it down. What does God want to teach us through these powerful words?

_____

_____

_____

_____

10

In the Shadow of the Shepherd

Dietrich Bonhoeffer Listened

Dietrich Bonhoeffer was a young German theologian during the rise of Hitler's Nazi regime prior to and during WWII. He was a brilliant preacher, teacher, and writer. He stood firm as the German church began to acquiesce to the Nazis. He wrote and taught that Christians must hold to the truth of the word. His teaching took him to Britain and the United States as well.

His writing and teaching made him an enemy of the German state. American believers urged him not to go back to Germany, but he returned. There he learned of the atrocities perpetrated by Hitler in the concentration camps, and this kind believer reluctantly joined others who unsuccessfully tried to eliminate Hitler.

Eventually his work was destroyed, his students were jailed or conscripted, and he was sent to a concentration camp. There he wrote, studied, and encouraged those around him. While imprisoned, evidence of the plot against Hitler was uncovered, and he was hung along with the others involved in the plot. This occurred only weeks before the Nazi regime collapsed and most of the Bonhoeffer family were killed during the war.

Among his writings are *The Cost of Discipleship* and *Letters and Papers from Prison*. Through his writing Dietrich Bonhoeffer continues to make disciples into this century. He is still showing us how a believer in the One True God lives in contentious times listening for the voice of the Shepherd.

Abigail, the Angel of Nabal's House Listened

Abigail is described by one author as the good angel of Nabal's household and one of the loveliest women in the Bible. She was both wise and kind. She was also beautiful. Wise, kind, beautiful . . .

Then there is her husband, Nabal.

This man was a piece of work. He was rich, rude, and rough. He was evil in his doings and filled with pride. Bless Abigail's heart; imagine what that meant for her. In David's encounter with this couple, the character of both Abigail and Nabal was revealed.

Nabal's shepherds were shearing their sheep and David and his men camped nearby. David's men protected the shepherds from their enemies as they went about their work. Then David sent some of his men to ask Nabal for food and provision. But Nabal insulted them and sent them away. Because hospitality is so significant in this culture, Nabal's rejection of David's men was a great offense. David overreacted to the situation vowing to kill Nabal's family and was headed there to do so when Abigail intervened.

The moment she heard what happened, she went into action to protect her family. She gathered food and provision to take to David and his men. When she reached David, she honored him by bowing down before him. Then she pled the case of her foolish husband, whose name, incidentally, means "foolish." Her plea before David revealed a lovely countenance and that she was a woman of discernment and wisdom. She told David, "As his name is, so is he. Nabal is his name and folly is with him." Abigail was successful in her intervention, and David relented.

When Abigail arrived home, foolish Nabal was giving a banquet and was drunk. This good woman in a bad marriage was listening to the voice of God and following Him. She had been planting seeds of faithfulness, perhaps for years. And without her realizing it, God was guiding her around that next curve—one that would entirely change her life. Within a few weeks, Nabal died and David took this amazing woman for his wife. She stepped out to protect her family and stopped the future king of Israel from killing out of anger, and then she married the guy. I love happy endings.

Dietrich Bonhoeffer was a man living in a troubled time. Abigail was a woman living in a troubled marriage. Yet each listened for the voice of God. Neither Dietrich nor Abigail let their extreme circumstances control their responses to life. One went to glory ministering the love of Jesus until the end. The other was left on this side of heaven to become the wife of the King of Israel. Both were in the shadow of the Shepherd and listening for His voice.

Just Follow Me

Maybe we have been hurt, disappointed or are dealing with difficult people. Perhaps we have great financial need or suffer with physical problems like Paul did. He asked God three times to heal his "thorn in the flesh." Yet God did not. God's reply to Paul might have gone like this: "I'm not going to heal your infirmity, my son. But I am going to give you grace sufficient to live with it, give thanks in it, and be content in Me as you, *with that infirmity,* draw others to the Truth. It's about the souls of men, son. Follow Me."

Maybe we have a disagreeable husband like Abigail. Maybe we are waiting for our extended family problems to be resolved, or for Mr. or Miss Right to sweep us off our feet. Perhaps we are facing persecution for our faith in Christ. If we have not yet faced persecution for following Jesus, at some point we will.

These very real circumstances are hard. Contentment in the Shepherd didn't mean that Bonhoeffer was not sad at times, afraid, or desiring his release from prison to return home. It did not mean that Abigail did not hope that her husband would become a godly man or that her days were not difficult. It meant that while they were in these circumstances they didn't waste their days. Lives were touched around him, and in both cases lives were saved.

Even with his infirmity Paul didn't let any grass grow under his feet. God used him to the end. While under house arrest in Rome, he influenced Caesar's household for Christ. The persecution against him led him to the very household whose posterity would perhaps influence the most lives. These ordinary people had learned the secret. Though we are not Bonhoeffer, Abigail, or Paul, we too can listen for the voice of the Shepherd, follow Him, and influence our world for eternity.

The Blood of the Martyrs

Years ago when I read *The Book of Martyrs* I was shocked and humbled at the courage of brothers and sisters through history who were killed for proclaiming their faith in Jesus Christ. Persecution for following Jesus is new to us, but not to most

Christians through the ages. As Tertullian proclaimed in the 9th century, "The blood of the martyrs is the seed of the church."

I never thought that during my lifetime I would see people in the United States begin to lose their religious freedoms, let alone see persecution against Christians across the globe more than any other time in history. Yet each year 40,000 Christians are reported killed for their faith. Many who are martyred are never reported, and those displaced, imprisoned, or tortured number far more.

Bonhoeffer must have grieved his world and his nation and what it was becoming, for the good stripped away with the bad. We are grieving, as well. We grieve for what our country could have been—what it may be again. This should not scare us to the corner though. The plight of our nation, the world, and especially the church should force us boldly to our knees.

There have been two spiritual awakenings in America's history and both were in contentious times. Perhaps God is shaking us from our complacency and comfort so we will pray for a third great awakening—getting us to Caesar's household. Christians are being martyred more than at any time in History, but more souls are coming to Christ in this century than at any other time in History as well. Maybe the Lord is just *rolling us over*.

Roll Over

God is in it. He is. He is showing us the way. He continues to show us who He is in *everything*! Like Paul through an unjust arrest and a shipwreck, God will get us to Caesar's household - wherever that is for us - if that is where He wants us. Maybe He is rolling us over.

From the time I was a child I have loved to sleep—early to bed, early to rise. I would roll over on my dominant left side, curl up in a ball and fall blissfully to sleep. This was my mode for sleep for forty years until I began to have back trouble and pain that kept me awake all night. Finally through trial and error I realized the only way to stop the pain was to become a back sleeper. A back sleeper! Really?

Yes, I had to roll over onto my back, put a pillow under my knees, and lie as straight and still as I could on a very hard bed. Then the pain stopped. It was so frustrating to me to realize that to sleep well again, I had to roll over.

Years later when I saw an x-ray of my back I understood why God had required this of me. My lower back is curved precariously to the left. And sleeping on my left side had exacerbated that curve, so my Shepherd *made* me roll over. I didn't like it. I was sad to have to change something I had been comfortable with all my life. I could in no way see around that curve. God could though, and He made me roll over.

Through circumstances that are uncomfortable, scary, and disheartening, God often times is *making* us roll over. He is taking that crook and pulling us to Himself so we will listen to His voice. He is challenging us to follow Him. He is urging us to keep the main thing the main thing, to pursue an intimate relationship with God that will draw our world to Him. Along with Paul, Dietrich Bonhoeffer, and Abigail, we *can* find contentment in contentious times as we learn and live the secret of which Paul wrote. These saints of God knew it was about God and His kingdom and the souls of men. They learned through contentious times that being content in the Lord did not mean life would be easy or that they would not hurt. It meant though, that they lived with purpose.

I continue to learn that as well. I started that fight for contentment when my husband left, when the money wouldn't make it to the end of the month, when the hand-me-downs were hand-me-downs, and when there were not enough hours in the day. I remember thinking, *How could I possibly be hearing the voice of God? Things are so hard,* and Bonhoeffer and Abigail might have thought that, too.

Jesus was right in the middle of God's will and was tempted by the deceiver. He was in the center of God's will and was led to the cross. So I got on my shaky knees and put my eyes on the Shepherd. My Shepherd made me roll over then and in sheer desperation I began to listen for His voice and to follow Him. It was remembering that my goal was to raise my boys to love Jesus and point my students to Him that gave me strength.

It didn't mean I was emotionless. We cry, we laugh, we dance, we mourn, we love passionately, and our hearts are broken at times. But the secret is to keep the eternal purpose in mind—to set our mind on things above in prayer.

Over those little men I prayed that they become Mighty men of God, not ordinary but extraordinary for Christ. I must have prayed that prayer a thousand of times. I forgot about it for some time, but after hearing a sermon on the radio I thought to myself, *Lady, you need to be praying that big ol' prayer again. Pray big and leave the results to God. That is what you are always telling people.*

Contentment starts in our hearts with the decision each *day* to trust that it is God who is leading us through our days, The God who gave His baby boy for us. Time with God is not ritual, not superstition, not just a prayer list, but keeps my heart fresh to the voice of the Holy Spirit.

Until We Step Over to the Other Side

When we are young we are so busy keeping the wheels on the bus that most of us have little time to think about future generations. But as we grow older we think about such things. I have thought what it will be like for my grandchildren and their children in the decades to come. If I, like many Christians around the world today, were sitting on the floor of a cold prison cell with my grandchildren around me, what would I offer them that is greater than me? Have I lived a life that has shown them that I listen for God's voice to lead me through my days? Does Grammy live with purpose? Does she have God's word in her? Does she have on her armor? Can she wield the sword? Is she secure in the shadow of her Shepherd?

Is Grammy content in Christ?

I so want the faces in front of me to see the powerful love of God pouring through me. That's what I am working toward by His Spirit and in Jesus' name. As I seek to live in light of the cross and its message following the voice of the Shepherd, no doubt I am going to find myself in touchy, even controversial situations. But my job description will not change. It will intensify.

I am here to fish.

Like others before us, our children and grandchildren who will follow us, and those in countries today who are persecuted or killed for their faith, this is the time to make the main thing the main thing. And the main thing from the garden remains the souls of men and women.

We are here to fish.

Therefore, we love the people in front of us each day. We remember that nothing is for nothing, and that every appointment is a divine appointment. We endeavor to remember that we have only a certain number of days and when God is through with us on this side, whether by accident, illness, or disaster, He will usher us to the "other side." We don't need to lose one night's sleep over when He takes us to heaven. In fact, it is none of our business.

So what do I want to do before that last day? What can I do? I can live with purpose.

In the high school, newly married, child rearing, single parent, never married, divorced, grieving loss, enduring illness, in need of healing, empty nester, the golden years, or that last toddling season of life—we have great purpose. It is profound that in God's sovereign will we start life as toddlers and finish the race toddling, as well. Our Shepherd carries us at the beginning of our life and is still carrying us at the end. No matter how fragile our bodies become we can continue to utter that simple cry even if only in our hearts. "Help me, Jesus." "Help them Jesus."

I will be leaning into one learning curve after another until in God's perfect time I will step over to the other side. In every season of life my relationship with God through prayer and believing His word has been a companion to contentment. I either fight my Shepherd's lead or I follow Him. It has always been my choice.

The Shepherd's Arms

For many years I have enjoyed peace knowing that God has numbered our days and that this life and death business is His business. But there was a time when my teenage boys were starting to drive that I was not content to leave those days and times to God. I prayed *and* I worried. At times as they headed out the door I would say, "God bless you! I love you! Watch out for the crazies!" I did want them to watch out for the crazy people out there. I did love them and wanted to bless them. But I was worried about them.

One afternoon in the spring of Parker's senior year of high school he headed out the door and across the yard like he had many of times before. But that day he said something to me I'll never forgot. Standing on the porch I proclaimed once again, "God bless you! I love you! Watch out for the crazies!" Knowing me well and sensing the concern in my voice Parker stopped short, turned around, and looked me squarely in the eye. Then he said kindly, "Remember, Momma, I'll see you sooner. Or I'll see you later." Parker reminded me that it was the Shepherd's arms that held him, not mine. It is the Shepherd's arms that hold You and yours as well—*especially* in these contentious times. That is the secret.

Learning the Secret

Psalm 23

The LORD is my shepherd,
    I shall not want.
He makes me lie down in green pastures;
    He leads me beside quiet waters.
He restores my soul;
    He guides me in the paths of righteousness
For His name's sake.
    Even though I walk through the valley of the shadow of death,
I fear no evil, for You are with me.
    Your rod and Your staff, they comfort me.
You prepare a table before me in the presence of my enemies;
    You have anointed my head with oil;
My cup overflows.
    Surely goodness and mercy will follow me all the days of my life.
And I will dwell in the house of the LORD forever. (NASB)

When I use my vertical letters to memorize Psalm 23, to meditate on what God is telling me, it absolutely transforms my heart. I encourage you to hide these words in your heart!

T	I	H	E	F	Y	Y	S	A
L	G	G	T	Y	P	H	G	I
I	P;	M	I	A	A	A	A	W
M	H	I	W	W	T	M	M	D
S	L	T	T	M.	B	H	S	I
I	M	P	T	Y	M	W	F	T
S	B	O	V	R	I	O;	M	H
N	S	R	O	A	T	M	A	O
W.	W.	F	T	Y	P	C	T	T
H	H	H	S	S	O	O.	D	L
M	R	N	O	T	M		O	F.
M	M	S.	D	C	E;		M	
T	S;		I	M.			L.	
L			F					
D			N					
			E,					

Psalm 23

- The Lord is my Shepherd (Is He?). (If He is) I want for nothing.

- The first thing is that He is going to make me rest. He makes me lie down in green pastures. In that rest He leads me beside the quiet waters and refreshes my soul. Making money, vacations, having a spouse, children, the right job or house . . . none of these strivings will refresh our souls.

- Only The Shepherd can refresh our souls. So we keep going back to him for refreshment because He will guide me along the right path for His name sake.

- Yes, He is guiding us with purpose. It's for the name of Christ. Your life and my life is lived for the name of Christ. We are Christians, little Christs. As I ponder those words I marvel that He is guiding me in paths that will make me more righteous for His name!

- As He guides me, I am at times going to be walking through the valley of the shadow of death. It is going to be scary; I am going to want to run away from the questions, the pain and fear, the hurt. But I will run to Him. I hold onto Him. Then I will fear no evil because I know He is right there with me - in me!

- Your rod and your staff they comfort me. His guidance, His drawing me to Himself, sometimes Him rolling me over even if I don't understand it or like it at the time, is ultimately for me.

- In preparing a table before me and anointing my head with oil, God honors and heals me. He loves and honors me even in the presence of those who count me as an enemy.

- He fills me up. God fills me up. So much that goodness and loving kindness will follow me all the days of my life, even over to the other side as I am with Him forever.

Philippians 4:4-8

Rejoice in the Lord always. I will say it again: Rejoice! [5] Let your gentleness be evident to all. The Lord is near. [6] Do not be anxious about anything, but in every situation, by prayer and petition, with thanksgiving, present your requests to God. [7] And the peace of God, which transcends all understanding, will guard your hearts and your minds in Christ Jesus.

[8] Finally, brothers and sisters, whatever is true, whatever is noble, whatever is right, whatever is pure, whatever is lovely, whatever is admirable—if anything is excellent or praiseworthy—think about such things.

R	L	A	R	H	I	A
I	Y	A	T	A	N,	I
T	G	A	G.	Y	W	E
L	B.	B	A	M	I	O
A.	E	I	T	I	R,	P-
I	T	E	P	C	W	T
W	A	S,	O	J.	I	A
S		B	G	F	P,	S
I	T	P	W	B	W	T.
A	L	A	T	A	I	
R!	I	P	A	S	L,	
	N.	W	U,	W	W	
	D	T,	W	I	I	
	N	P	G	T,	A-	
	B	Y	Y	W	I	

Philippians 4:4-8

Dear Father, we want to stay under the watchful care of our Shepherd being content in Him alone. May our hearts be broken for the broken. May we respond to Your call to pray and live in the word of God so we will be faithful in season and out of season. By Your Spirit and in the power of God that raised Jesus from the dead, may we be content in Christ alone, and may our contentment speak God's love to our world.

In Jesus' name. Amen

About Dana Gailey

Dana Gailey, a lifelong educator, has a passion for Jesus, children, and teaching God's truths to anyone who will listen. Being a mother and grandmother has been her greatest joy.

She is married to Don Gailey and their blended family consists of seven children and a gaggle of grandchildren. She and Don live in North Texas.

Contact Dana at danagailey3@gmail.com.

Made in the USA
Columbia, SC
04 April 2022

58380592R00109